VOGUE

MORE DASH

BOOK CLUB ASSOCIATES
LONDON

THAN CASH

KATE HOGG

For William

BOOK CLUB ASSOCIATES
LONDON

This edition published 1982 by
Book Club Associates by arrangement
with Hutchinson & Co. (Publishers) Ltd

First Published 1982
Reprinted 1983
© Kate Hogg and The Condé Nast Publications Ltd 1982

Set in Photina

Printed in England by Balding + Mansell Limited
and bound by Wm Brendan & Son Ltd, Tiptree, Essex

CONTENTS

INTRODUCTION

This book is about fashion in its most modern context, based on the belief that today the individual inside the clothes is much more important than the statement made by her outward appearance. In the sixties and seventies your appearance spoke for you. For the image conscious, almost compulsory fashions provided a security that masked the wearer's originality, and in many ways made life a lot easier, eliminating that essential ingredient of contemporary style – personal choice.

Now the reasons behind your choice of clothes is determined by what *you* like, what suits you and what feels right – no more the ritual, overserious performance of becoming a fashion dummy and letting the clothes take over. Today it is definitely more of a compliment for other people to remember you as the girl with a great sense of humour, than as the girl in bright yellow bloomers. Of course what you wear does matter enormously. It is no use pretending that other people are not impressed or attracted by a striking appearance. They may never have discovered your sparkling conversation or dry wit, were it not for your pink satin dancing shoes. But equally they may well be put off or intimidated when confronted by an overpoweringly fashion-conscious person who seems more involved in her own image than getting through to anyone else.

The concept of more-dash-than-cash dressing goes beyond the obvious army-surplus, jumble-sale or ethnic fashion alternatives; the kind of looks which do provide (when well put together) an instant bargain style, but plunge people who don't feel at home in khaki, battered tweeds or peasant skirts into deep depression and drive them back into mediocre chain-store outfits. Happily the idea of budget style need never be limited to anti-fashion themes. There are many other accessible and wearable options to take from the mainstream, more classic side of fashion.

But however individual your style of dress, it is impossible to escape from certain key fashion rules. Most of the etiquette dos and don'ts (when to wear hats, gloves, match your accessories, be seen in skirts and not trousers) are now outdated. But the stock phrases that repeatedly advise a well-balanced, colour-coordinated wardrobe, that stress the value of good quality long-term buys, and the importance of carefully chosen accessories, are infuriatingly still true and well worth acknowledging – hence their inclusion in this book.

Another syndrome that is a mainstay of the stock fashion vocabulary is 'quality'. It is usually synonymous with expensive luxury dressing, but here more-dash-than-cash quality describes the best of a type. Instead of scrimping on the cheapest edition of an expensive product, it can be more effective to splash out on the grandest alternative at a lower price level. On the basis that it is more satisfying to splurge within a safe price range at a good café than toy with the hors d'oeuvres and dread the bill in a smart restaurant, there is no point trying to live up to certain financial standards if you cannot afford to carry them through without a deprived struggle. Remember that a top quality wool coat looks far more luxurious than a mean fur jacket, and instead of tinny gold plate jewellery, it makes sense to choose beautifully made wooden beads.

The options for personal appearance have never been so diverse. As there is no longer a definitive last word that sets guidelines of what is 'in' or 'out', so it is more difficult to find the right balance between the extremes of either overdoing or completely abandoning the idea of fashion. Now that so many people are bewildered by the confusion of the latest styles, the extremists, who sometimes look positively ugly, are admired more for their outrageousness than for the actual charm of their clothes, while their opposites, who discard fashion, seem to use economy as a lame excuse, blaming hard times instead of a total lack of effort for their unimaginative appearance. Making the effort to look more striking costs very little. A fresh attitude and energy are more vital than money.

Much of the fashion talk in this book concerns the everyday basics that belong in most wardrobes. It is not a catalogue of new looks to rush out and buy; a different approach to what you already possess can be just as effective as an extravagant shopping spree. Imagination, a sense of challenge and self-motivation are the essential accompaniments to this book – it contains guidelines as inspirations and ideas, not as rigid instructions.

Although this book is about contemporary fashion, the photographs prove how some styles survive the passing of time. Drawn from a span of over ten years, they illustrate, except for the shortlived gimmick pictures, how timeless and unquestionably economical the best of fashion can be.

AN INDIVIDUAL STYLE

Success with today's fashion relies far more on individual style than a large budget. But because style is not a concrete quality, it can be a daunting phenomenon. Although style can be recognized, like a talent for cooking or singing, it cannot be analysed as there is no set formula to follow. It would be like laying down rules for every person's character. Style is part of a personality and, like every other trait, is unique to each person. Everybody has *a* style, just as everybody has some sense of humour; what counts is whether it is an original and true style; whether it comes naturally and feels right. It is like an instinctive sixth sense to make the best of yourself.

Good style is based on the confidence that comes from a positive attitude when you have the conviction to be yourself. People with true style exude self-assurance because they feel completely secure about themselves. They have an inner flair which gives them the knack of making whatever they wear look terrific, always exactly right for the occasion, never contrived or self-consciously perfect. They are the kind of irritating people who stand out in a room, not because of any outrageous clothes – in fact they often make others feel uncomfortably overdressed – but because of a special, indefinable presence. You often remember their personality or conversation more distinctly than their fashion. It is immediate proof that there is far more to style than clever clothes.

The foundation of self-confidence becomes a springboard for originality. Stylish people often have the nerve to be innovators. The instant reaction is to copy their style but, unlike a specific fashion, style is more difficult to follow. Like a house interior, style goes beyond the immediate appearance and the objects and colours in the rooms. If you transplant the interior design from one style of house into another, it looks out of place. The personality of the owners, the atmosphere and type of house are an integral part of the charm. Each one complements

Success with today's fashion relies on individual style and originality

the other. The starting point is to come to terms with yourself; to realize that you are only going to feel comfortable in clothes that suit your personality. You won't achieve style if you try to camouflage yourself in contradicting fashions, however much you love them on other people. It turns the idea of fashion into a battle of wills. If you try to be somebody different you can never relax and feel in tune with your appearance. You cannot learn style like a foreign language, but you can become aware of people who automatically stand out, and try to determine why they are special. They are not necessarily great beauties, but they do have a certain allure.

The guideline for an original style is to follow your own instincts. Once you establish a strong feeling for your own style, there is nothing wrong with taking inspiration from other people, providing you realize that no two people can or should want to look identical. You cannot copy, but you can adapt the ideas. On the basis that style relies more on how rather than what you wear, adapting ideas is not copying – it is more a matter of individual interpretation.

The first criterion of good style, of whatever kind, is consistency. Even if the person you admire is unpredictable, she is consistently so. Having a style is about being independent, letting a personal feeling evolve. It is essential to keep fashion in perspective, not to let it rule your life. It should never be taken too seriously. It is something to have fun with, to make you feel wonderful, not worried. Style is no longer synonymous with self-conscious 'dressing up' where everything matches and co-ordinates, and where there is never a hair out of place.

You can have style with whatever type of fashion you choose to follow. The trouble is that without firm guidelines of what to wear, the easiest solution is to muddle along looking mediocre and much the same as everybody else. It feels safer. The humiliation at school was intense when everyone wore regulation jerseys and you stuck out with a (probably far prettier) home-made one. Like uniform, middle-of-the-road clothes provide a safe anonymity which is a dangerous niche to slide into. It is more comfortable to go with the crowd than risk the embarrassment of looking different and being stared at. But it is essential to step out of the standard mould to be an individual. People only stare because they recognize, and wish they had, the nerve and ingenuity to be more original. When you feel confident and proud of your appearance you can safely assume that most second glances and turning heads can be taken as compliments.

So how do you set about being a fashion individual? The over-whelming variety of clothes that confronts you in a shop can be daunting, but it need never be limiting. There is no excuse for everyone to look the same, even in a small town. Common sense is the first guideline. Choose clothes that fit your lifestyle and give you the best value for money – in terms of how often you can wear them, and how well they work with the rest of your wardrobe. This may sound simplistic, but there is a lot of truth in the idea that the clothes you love and long to own should, within reason, be the ones that suit you best. Buying something because you think it is a good investment can be a waste. It treats fashion as a commodity like sugar and salt or stocks and shares. Everything you own should make you feel good, not just sensible.

Common sense should be used on a more practical level. It is pointless to invest in clothes which you can't afford the time or money to maintain. Don't buy the kind of clothes that need regular dry-cleaning if your budget does not stretch that far. It is shortsighted to opt for a smart, groomed image if you do not have the energy to carry it through. Establish a style of fashion that works around you, not one that rules your life, and you will find a thread of unity running through your wardrobe. The plaintive 'I've got nothing to wear' cry should fade into the past.

The idea that you need plenty of money to look distinctive is an outdated concept. There are advantages in a small budget. It forces you to be disciplined, to think hard about how much you really want every article you buy. A large wardrobe can be more of a hindrance than a help; the wider the choice, the harder it is to establish a consistent style. Wearing different clothes every day is not a sign of being well dressed.

Time is more important than a large budget. What counts is *how* you wear clothes; not just whether you put a belt round a sweater, but the condition and appearance of everything you put on. The seemingly insignificant details become finishing touches that make all the difference between an undistinguished and a striking impression. It does involve effort, but it is an approach that soon becomes second nature. Find time to look after your clothes; however inexpensive they may be, they deserve proper treatment. Whether you live in jeans and tee shirts, jumble-sale finds or tailored separates, the same standards apply. Wearing casual clothes is no reason to be scruffy. Treat everything you own as if it cost five times its price. A basic rule is to follow cleaning or laundering instructions on every single garment. The quickest way to spoil clothes is to throw them in a washing machine at the wrong temperature or to ignore the 'dry clean only' labels.

Ironing can be a bore but it is vital. Nothing ruins an appearance so much as crumpled, unpressed clothes. If you measure the time it takes to iron a shirt against the crisp impact it creates, the effort is worthwhile. Have an ironing board set up permanently, ideally, where you dress, so that everything can be pressed before it goes on. Some clothes, especially crease-prone cotton and linen, need ironing every time you wear them,

Even when you do spend hours deciding what to wear, create the impression of an effortless, unrehearsed appearance

Accessory impact: one luxurious muffler can make all the difference to everyday basics

not just after each wash. Ironing time can be cut down if clothes are stored properly; skirts and trousers kept on clip-top hangers, not folded on wire coat hangers. If you have the space, hanging shirts reduces the creases. Knitwear should always be folded flat, as hanging encourages it to sag out of shape. Coats, jackets and dresses look much better if they are kept on wooden or padded hangers, instead of wire ones. Don't adopt the attitude that second best is good enough today and you will do something about it tomorrow. If you care about your appearance, you owe it to yourself to look good all the time, however tired you may feel. Fate has a nasty habit of making you bump into somebody important when you have dirty hair, tights with holes, a sweater darned in clashing wool, a jacket with buttons missing and scuffed shoes.

It is difficult to lay down rules about how much to spend on clothes and how to spread a budget. Now that fashion is such a personal choice, there are no set values of what is a good or sensible buy. When fashion was predictable it was easier to work out a spending scale. You needed a sensible coat, useful day dresses, an evening gown, and enough set aside for hats, gloves, shoes and underwear. But now the priorities are whatever you want them to be. It is essential to be open-minded and to rethink the price scale when necessary. Shake off drummed-in notions that certain garments like a coat, an evening dress, a jacket, justify a high price, while it is extravagant to spend the same amount or more on shoes, knitwear, belts and other accessories. When you mix different price levels your success depends on unexpected combinations. It is more original to add a marvellous belt to a cheap dress, than to spoil the effect of an expensive dress with a plastic belt. It is not immoral if the belt costs more than the dress – no one else will know the financial breakdown of your outfit. A great accessory is still sadly underrated. It can stamp ordinary clothes with individuality.

Look at clothes from a fresh angle, uncoloured by what you expect to pay and see. When you have style you never accept anything as it comes. You switch it around: with old surplus trousers, swop gym shoes for bright red sandals; promote a Shetland sweater into something special by adding a white cashmere muffler that costs twice the price of the Shetland; transform a boy's shirt by adding antique shell buttons. You are never happy to be ordinary, everything has to be a little different – not pretentious but original and seemingly effortless. Even if you do spend three hours deciding what to wear, the trick is to create an impression that your appearance is quite unrehearsed – that everything happened quite by chance when you threw a few old things together.

The most versatile clothes are those that are simplest and least detailed, since it is impossible to stamp a style on anything already too gimmicky or exaggerated. Fashion is no longer something you have to

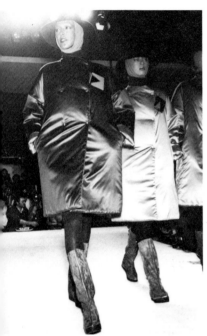

keep up with. It is not that fashion stands still, just that there are many more options to choose. There are no rigid divisions between fashions, nothing to stop you wearing a skirt from two winters ago with a new jacket if it looks and feels right.

The fashion cycle is like an enormous, slow-moving wheel with several smaller, fast-moving wheels turning in the same direction, but at different speeds. They represent the sudden, short-lived trends that come and go, looks that create instant images but leave their mark on mass-produced, chain-store fashion. To a high-fashion purist, the commercialized versions miss the main point of the story – the immediateness of it all. By the time the message of new shapes, proportions, colours or prints filters through to alerted high street stores, most dedicated followers are well into their next phase. High fashion in its most extreme undiluted form becomes a complete package, a look with a ready-made image. Accepting every craze as it comes along is a form of escapism. It is essential to be discerning; instinct tells you when you are in the wrong clothes. Like every kind of craze, high fashion begins to pall when the novelty fades. It is not worth splashing out on expensive versions every time a new one arrives on the scene, unless you really feel at home in one particular look. When something feels right, it usually suits your style, so take the opportunity to build an image from there and abandon the other gimmicks on the wheel.

There is no final word in fashion; there is not one grand hierarchy sending down memos about shapes and colours each season. The whole fashion world is jostling with ideas on every rung of its two-way ladder, which move up and down influencing different levels on their way. At the top are the couture collections: the most extravagant and isolated area of fashion – made-to-measure clothes for people who can afford the staggering prices. The ready-to-wear scene is more influential and faster moving. Twice a year in London, Paris, Milan and New York, designers show their collections to the press and store buyers. Like the couture shows, you expect a certain signature from each designer, and for each collection to be a natural progression from the last.

Although designers work in secrecy, they often seem to think on the same wavelength. Each season it is uncanny how a fashion message emerges from their collections. The first impression is that each one has been given the same theme and colour range for their inspiration, but when you look again, each collection bears the unmistakable stamp of its creator. Besides the mainstream, there are tributaries of different styles, particular to individual designers, or even countries. Paris fashion may be full of mini skirts, Milan awash with ankle-length trousers, and the most important idea in New York might be a new kind of jacket. The overall feeling is established by key points; the shape of the silhouette, new proportions, lengths, accessories, colours, prints and textures.

The ready-to-wear collections are an important source of inspiration for high street fashion. Trends are interpreted and redesigned to suit mass production. But success hangs on the style of the prototype – on whether it translates into a cheaper copy without losing its point. The charm of an intricate cut, a mix of textures, subtle colours and special details tends to get lost on the way. The ingenuity of buyers for fashion stores and boutiques varies enormously. Some can be relied upon to find a good interpretation which will appear in their stores at the same time, or only a fraction after, the original arrives in the designer boutique. Customers must be discerning and accept 'knock-off' fashion for what it is. The simplest major shapes – the trousers, skirts, coats – are often hardest to reproduce because they rely on an expert cut which is unsuitable for large-scale production. Instead, it can be easier to imitate the most exaggerated and bold shapes, but unless they are cleverly interpreted, these can become badly distorted. They may catch the message of the original but have little value in their own right.

In spite of their secrecy, it is surprising how designers think along the same lines. A crop of satin quilts in Italy; by Valentino, Fendi and Basile (left)

Unmistakable handwriting – the immaculate stamp of a Saint Laurent suit

Ready-to-wear originals are an important source of high street inspiration: but cheap imitations often fail as designer fashions rely on expensive materials, an intricate cut and subtle colouring. So borrow the spirit of the look instead, and put your own interpretation together – inspired perhaps by a Perry Ellis highwayman (left) or a Kenzo sailor (right)

The country look, Italian style at Gianni Versace. Track down your own from more traditional sources

Dissect each new designer fashion: recognize the simple white vests at Zoran, New York (opposite). *There is nothing to stop you improvising*

It is wiser to capture the spirit of the clothes than the details. This may be nautical – full of matelot tee shirts, sailor tops, white trousers and navy jackets; military – with uniforms, camouflage colours, medals and combat jackets; Scottish – with tartans, tam o'shanters and sporran bags; cowboys in denim, lumberjack shirts and fringed suede or Romantic in sprigged cotton frocks, white ruffles and lace; whatever the spirit, the message *you* pick up should be an impressionistic one.

If you take a general theme for your individual inspiration, it is not necessary to buy the expensive designer versions. It is quite possible to make your own look out of the genuine article. Instead of designer cowboys, go to the nearest Western store; instead of Kenzo sailors, make your own rig from proper nautical clothes. If there is a country look, be wary of high-priced fashion tweeds. Track down better quality classics from traditional outfitters and find your checked shirts in boys' departments, not boutiques. Dissect a fashion look; occasionally there will be simple shapes that you recognize, an ordinary white shirt or plain, round-neck sweater, for example. They are bound to be expensive because they carry designer labels, but there is nothing to stop you improvising.

The ready-to-wear fashion filters down the fashion ladder at different speeds and strengths. The alternative system works with the looks that start at street level and are gradually translated into commercial, mass fashion. This process is less alternative than it might seem. To begin with, it usually has an anti-fashion identity as a symbol of nonconformity associated with a particular cult. The punk movement is an example: it started as an aggressive reaction against society and turned into a commercially exploited fashion. Top designers removed it from its origins and punk became posh, to the fury of its originators.

Then there are looks which move from fringe level into everyday fashion, not so much a cult engineered by fortune hunters, more a case of good timing. The quest for a fit, healthy body prompted a demand for fashionable exercise clothes. Boundaries between sport and fashion wear have dissolved, and traditional athletic shapes – tracksuits, racing swimwear, running singlets, sweatshirts and leotards – appear regularly in fashion collections. The anti-fashion inspirations tend to surface as a reflection of hard times. When there is a recession, escapism is more fun than facing up to reality. It is easier to look backwards and sideways than straight ahead, so fashion dives into nostalgia. Anything old is more desirable than anything new, whether it is antique white lace underwear, thirties knitwear, fitted forties suits, rock and roll skirts or psychedelic minis. Sideways fashion leans into government surplus uniforms, ethnic originals or menswear. Inevitably the demand for these escapist clothes grows and inflates prices out of all proportion. Not

Anti-fashion cults often reflect hard times, when escapism is more inviting than reality. Nostalgia rules (right and left)*: a careful jumble of menswear and second-hand clothes, sharpened with some inevitable high fashion tweeds*

surprisingly, irony strikes again as crafty manufacturers take advantage of prevailing 'non-fashion' and produce relatively inexpensive versions to fill the demand. These commercial interpretations may appeal to a less discriminating shopper, but invariably spell instant death to the look for its instigators. Escapist fashions thrive on a rarity value that no copy can match in style or quality. Once mass produced and widely accessible, the elite concept of an alternative style dissolves into a gimmick.

WARDROBE TACTICS

Too many people limit their fashion scope by separating their wardrobe into compartments. Habit and tradition divide winter, summer, day, evening, holiday, town and country clothes into unrelated segments of a total wardrobe. There is an inbuilt fixation that it is wrong to mix clothes bought for different seasons and occasions. Rethink that attitude and look at a wardrobe as a united whole. Not that everything needs to match or come from the same shop; you should be able to see your wardrobe like a family, where everything is related to each other, some elements closely, others more distantly.

Traditional men's fashion is a good example of well-balanced dressing. Because of their limitations and more rational approach to clothes, men, even very image-conscious ones, seem to work on a smaller wardrobe scale, based on logic and necessity; they collect clothes with a long-term approach. Like the argument against a large budget, a small wardrobe encourages a consistent individual style more naturally than an extensive wardrobe of unrelated categories.

With a 'capsule' wardrobe the key has to be versatility. You need maximum options from the minimum amount of clothes. A guideline is how you pack a suitcase (not a trunk) that covers every possible eventuality. Limited space forces forward planning and precise organization, and you prune the selection down to versatile and favourite separates. Necessity may force you to improvise and mix clothes together more inventively than you would at home. If you stay longer than expected, and the only remaining clean shirt happens to be a ruffled silk 'evening' one, then you wear it with jeans and a cardigan in the day and you change in the evening by adding some beads to a lambswool V-neck sweater. Limitation stretches your imagination.

Separates provide more scope for individuality than ready-made, coordinated outfits. A suit, a jacket with a skirt or trousers, is fine if both halves work independently as well. It is a limiting buy if the top or bottom

Even one simple sweater can provide a surprising number of options

Seasonless basics (right) *to wear all year round*

Versatile mixes: (below) *satin with tweed and Shetland makes the look work day or night*

A subtle change: (opposite) *dressing up a cardigan with silk trousers*

Night switch: (above) *adding jewellery and hair ribbon spells evening*

look disjointed apart from the other. Well-balanced separates create the backbone of a capsule wardrobe. For maximum versatility they need to be as seasonless and as timeless as possible, so buy clothes in materials that do not restrict their life to a few months of the year. Light wools, corduroy, jersey, suede, brushed or knitted cotton, make more sense than very thick or fine materials. Timeless separates are clothes that can be dressed up or down to suit the time of day or situation.

The days of compulsory dressing up in formal evening clothes are gone; the attitude towards what to wear at night is now completely relaxed. There is still a contrast to make between day and evening dressing, but it does not rely on dressing-up as much as it does on a more subtle change. It is possible to make clothes work day and night by putting them together in a different way. One touch that spells evening can transform the look: it may be a flash of intense colour from an unusual accessory, extra sparkle from a piece of jewellery, or shine from bright leather sandals.

An element of surprise is effective, especially unexpected combinations of colour and material. When you mix grey flannel trousers with a satin blouse, a Shetland sweater with silk trousers, denim jeans with a silk camisole – the look progresses from day into night. The most basic separates take on new life in unexpected colours; an everyday cardigan becomes something special in pure white or delicate pastels. On the same lines there is something wonderfully throwaway about a glamorous crepe de Chine or silk satin in a subtle, understated pearl grey or beige.

A BASIC WARDROBE

Essential ingredients perform in more than one way. A simple, well-cut **shirt** in cotton or silk not only looks as good with jeans as it does at night with a taffeta skirt, but also as a loose summery jacket, or belted like a tunic.

One underrated basic is a plain white **tee shirt**, round or V-neck. It is an invaluable neutral garment, particularly in summer when it can take you through the day and night. Providing it is white and not yellowing, it looks good with jeans, shorts, skirts, dungarees, tailored or sporty jackets

Essential ingredients: a well-cut shirt or two, in cotton or silk

during the day, and can be dressed up at night with a striking necklace and a pretty skirt or silky trousers. In winter, tee shirts provide an extra layer: a round-neck worn under a brightly coloured V-neck sweater is a change from the predictable shirt collar.

A comprehensive **sweater collection** is essential. Shetland, lambswool, cotton knit and cashmere are investments which, well chosen, never lose their appeal or versatility. A plain V-neck, crew-neck or round-necked 'golfer' cardigan is much more useful than an uncoordinated assortment of fashionable sweaters covered in details or fancy stitches. The key to sweater dressing is the combination of plain shapes with a rich selection of colours and textures. Each sweater must work in its own right, but also add mileage to other separates. For instance, a plain lambswool V-neck can be worn on its own, or over a classic shirt, a tee shirt, a crew-neck sweater, a polo neck, or underneath a V-neck cardigan as a twinset. The twinset image is still unjustly regarded as dowdy, but the principle of a matching cardigan and short-sleeve sweater is an example of flexible dressing. Put your own twinsets together – but with a difference. Experiment with identically coloured sweaters in different thicknesses, a chunky, primrose wool cardigan over a fine, primrose wool slipover. Or try a lambswool twinset in highly contrasting or subtle colour combinations – black with white, or honey beige with cream. There are more options if your sweaters are not all the same size. A mansize, ribbed sweater can be worn casually over trousers, or on its own as a knitted mini dress with coloured tights. Neat-fitting sweaters are definitely smarter looking, especially if worn with a belt. There is nothing to stop you turning cardigans and V-necks back to front if the shape is suitable. It could be your surprise switch from day to night.

When it comes to vital mainstay **separates** – a jacket, skirts, trousers, maybe a coat – look for good quality. Paying slightly more than you would normally can be justified: you need value for money, and you cannot expect one cheap pair of trousers to replace the wear of three pairs without looking tatty and shapeless rather quickly. If you want something to last, the quality of the material and cut are crucial. You do have to grit your teeth and pay for a good fit. With tailored clothes, the quality and fit stand out, and any imperfections in the cut are emphasized. But fitting should not mean constricting. Good tailoring means clothes that are softly structured, not awkward to wear. If you cannot afford the price of a tailored style, choose less fitted clothes where the expertise of the cut is not so critical.

A **jacket** can be the most useful coordinating link. It gives unity to separates dressing without the uniformity of a matching suit. Style, colour and fabric should be as versatile and neutral as possible without being boring. A jacket has to add a lift, not just be a top layer. Simple

White tee shirts are invaluable year-round basics

Sweater dressing: the simplest shapes guarantee greater versatility

(Opposite) a well-chosen jacket can be a vital coordinating link in your basic wardrobe

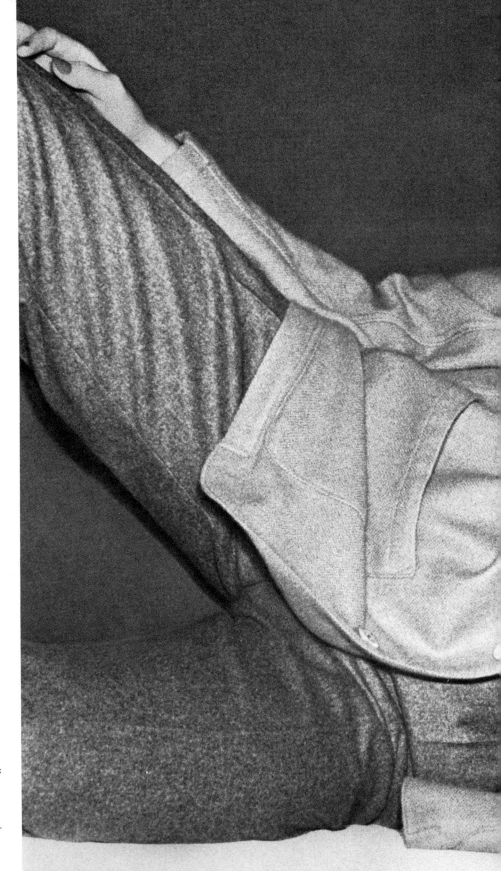

Jackets are useful during in between weather; an obvious bridge for spring/summer and autumn/winter dressing, when it is not cold enough for a coat, or warm enough to go without. And a jacket is not just for wearing outside; it has an inside life in cold weather, and can be worn like a cardigan over a shirt or sweater

styles free from superfluous fashion notes are essential. The shape itself depends on personal choice; perhaps a traditional blazer, a double-breasted boxy jacket, a cropped, bellboy collarless jacket, a jean or knitted blouson, a hooded parka or a classic windcheater. Whatever the shape, there are key points to check: avoid an exaggerated collar and revers, wide shoulders, unnecessary stitching or contrast piping, large pockets, and drawstring waists, hems or cuffs which tend to look messy, and change buttons that look cheap or too obvious. Provided the weight of the material is correct (wise choices are wool gaberdine, suiting, knitted wool, flannel, suede, leather, denim), jackets serve a year-round purpose. They are invaluable for inbetween weather, and a useful bridge between spring/summer and autumn/winter dressing when it is not cold enough for a coat, or warm enough to go without. A jacket is not just for wearing outside; it has an inside life in cold weather and can be worn like a cardigan over a shirt or sweater.

Have a balanced number of **skirts and trousers** for variety. Trousers can be made to look as smart as a skirt. The belief that a girl can only be dressed up if she wears a skirt has gone. The only relevant guideline is that cheap skirts can be made to look better than cheap trousers. The cut of a skirt is not quite as crucial as the cut and fit of trousers, especially if they are in a material like flannel, tweed, corduroy, or even denim. As a general rule heavier materials justify a higher price because you are

Basic proportions: heel heights and hemlines are closely related; fashions for short skirts and flat shoes often coincide

Everyday jackets: (below) *a denim blouson,* (right) *tartan-lined combat jacket. Trouser shapes* (far right) *where quality really matters*

*A coat should be a classic –
completely timeless with
minimum fashion detail*

*A raincoat is a seasonless
alternative. Choose a traditional
shape that accumulates style as it
ages*

paying, you hope, for a good shape. Lightweight cotton adapts more successfully into inexpensive, loosely cut drawstring or elasticated trousers and skirts.

To find a trouser shape that suits your figure you usually have to try many different shapes. Unless you are extremely thin, skintight trousers in a firm material can look unflattering and uncomfortable. Stretch Lycra, shiny Spandex or stretch denim are better for very tight trousers because they do at least move with the body. The most useful and flattering shape is the simplest: a straight-legged trouser softened with two front pleats at the waist. Trouser shapes are no longer a fashion law, but extreme styles look ridiculous when the craze passes.

With skirts, moving hemlines count more than shapes. Basic styles – straight, pencil slim, wrapped, pleated, kilted, tiered, or dirndl – seldom go out of fashion. What does change are the proportions. Finding the right length for the right shape is essential. Hemlines can range from above the knee to above the ankle, it is a case of balancing the shape of the skirt to the most flattering leg length and to what you will wear with it. A common mistake is to wear straight skirts too long; the best length is mid or just below the knee; anything longer looks dowdy, dated, and out of proportion. Fuller or tiered skirts can be worn longer, as they have the fullness to balance the extra length. Heel heights and hemlines are closely related. Shorter skirts look best with lower heels (fashions for minis and flat shoes usually coincide), longer skirts need the elegance of high heels. Skirt options can be stretched by doubling up on summer and evening styles. Cotton, tiered peasant skirts in bright colours can be dressed up with warm tights and a pretty angora cardigan for winter evenings.

Buying a **coat** is a substantial outlay in any wardrobe, one choice where real value for money is essential. Value in terms of wear: you must be able to live in it for at least six months of the year. It has to work with all your clothes and meet every demand, without being too smart or too scruffy for certain occasions. A coat should be a classic – simple and timeless. Any style that is a fashion statement is limiting. It is remarkable how the traditional, understated cut of a man's overcoat never looks out of place. There is nothing exaggerated or pretentious about the classic double-breasted line, the immaculately proportioned collar, revers and pockets. It is an example of perfect simplicity. The key that turns a basically masculine shape into a feminine coat is softer, less structured tailoring. But a winter coat is not an essential buy; it is better to go without if you cannot find one you love. A **raincoat**, especially one with a detachable warm lining, can take its place. It needs the performance of a winter coat, plus a seasonless quality that fits your clothes all year round, not just in the rain. Well-worn raincoats have much more style than

brand-new looking ones, but you do need the right shape to start with: the traditional trench coat or single-breasted mac. Fashion raincoats look tatty, not stylish, after five years.

Accessories cannot be counted as part of the wardrobe backbone, but they do qualify for an important share of the budget. They bring change and variety to a limited range of clothes. Without a choice of accessories a mathematical style can become monotonous. As they have such diverse tasks to perform they can be divided into basic accessories and switch accessories. **Basics** are everyday essentials like shoes, belts and a bag, which for practical and economical reasons have to work in shape and colour with all your clothes. **Switch accessories** are vital extras that transform one set of clothes from being casual to dressed up, or from day to evening. They set a mood. It may be the addition of a beautiful necklace, a pair of drop earrings, an armful of copper bangles, a bronze leather sash, or a switch from moccasins to high-heeled sandals.

A change of **shoes** is the most obvious way to dress a look up or down. They spell a mood more instantly than any other accessory, and for that reason it is essential to treat them with the importance they deserve. They should never be an afterthought: the wrong shoes with new clothes ruin the effect completely. The key point is quality. Unfortunately leather and suede are expensive but it is worth saving up for one good leather pair rather than buying several cheap pairs. Cheap shoes are false economy. A well-cared-for leather pair will look smart long after cheaper ones fall apart. Suede is labelled as impractical and hard to maintain which is untrue. Providing it is protected immediately against the rain, it is no more difficult to care for than leather.

Each pair needs to be versatile enough for more than one kind of occasion. Some have a year-round life. Summer sandals can double as evening shoes, low-heeled loafers look as good with bare legs in summer as they do with thick socks in winter. Shoe versatility does not mean limiting the colour choice to black, brown or navy. Bright colours are just as useful and more seasonless than dark wintry shades. If you cannot afford leather or suede shoes, it is wiser to find a material that is not an obvious imitation: choose brightly coloured sporty canvas shoes or espadrilles, velvet slippers or satin dancing pumps.

Bags are often more of an afterthought than shoes. The idea of spending a lot of money on one bag for each outfit is ludicrous. One or two bags should be enough to fit with all your clothes. There is no need for a bag to match your clothes or shoes, it simply needs to be in keeping. Do not fall into the trap of buying a bag in predictable useful colours like brown, navy, burgundy or black which look out of place with light summer clothes, especially if the bag is a large holdall type. As with shoes, a bright red or blue can be more versatile and original, but the

A change of shoes is a way to dress a look up or down. A pair of high-heeled sandals with these same clothes would switch a holiday look into something smarter and more elegant

most infallible seasonless colours are shades of beige, grey and khaki. A smaller bag looks smarter and goes with more day and night looks than an enormous sack, which in the evening can look like an overnight suitcase. The alternative is to keep a little zip or knotted purse to hold evening essentials inside the large bag. Some of the best shapes are borrowed from bags with a practical purpose, like the school satchel, duffel bag, or a flat clutch like a man's briefcase or wallet. Unlike shoe shopping it is easy to find cheap alternatives to leather or suede; low-priced materials like canvas, parachute nylon, webbing, raffia, tapestry, wood, even cardboard. In desperation, a straw basket looks far better than plastic leather.

When it comes to balancing finances, one critical area that is too often overlooked or hard done by is **underwear**. It is not an overstatement to say that what goes underneath is just as important as what goes on top. Badly fitting or badly shaped underwear can ruin the final effect – however well put together the clothes may be. Take time to shop around and find underwear, especially bras, that suit your figure. Many people wear a wrong size or incorrectly fitted bra. Even if the prospect sounds daunting, it is worth being properly measured and fitted by a trained saleslady who will check the strap adjustments and cup size if you know yourself to be inbetween standard chain-store or brand sizes. A common mistake is to shorten the straps which pulls up the back of the bra and pushes the bust forward unnaturally.

Underwear ridges caused by bulges from tight pants are another terrible letdown for appearance. The answer is to wear a larger size, but make sure they lie smooth, or to find shapes that enhance the outer garment. It may mean something more substantial than tiny bikini briefs, but more surface area does not imply heavy-duty corsets. The latest foundationwear fabrics are light and comfortable with subtle stretch properties for smoothing stomachs and hips. Under fitted trousers and jeans, eliminate the chance of a ridge by wearing waist-level boxer pants with high cut legs. The best solution is to investigate the wide range of styles yourself, but don't be put off if you are directed to the corsetry department, it doesn't mean what it says any more.

In the hosiery department, the variety of brands and types of **stockings and tights** is confusing, but it is one area where it is definitely worth paying a little extra for quality. There are two criteria (apart from colour) to consider: the texture and the denier. Fine-knit tights have a much better appearance and a more uniform colour than micromesh; they are smoother to touch and unfortunately more expensive. Sheer tights range between thirty, twenty, fifteen, ten and even seven denier. The finest fifteen and ten deniers, which predictably are the most expensive, do look much more elegant than the thicker twenty and thirty deniers (seven

Colour sense: (opposite) *each neutral spectrum is a base for coordinating bright, pastel and subtle colours.*
Try white as a summer neutral with lifts of scarlet, pale blue and bronze

(Next spread left) *the beige spectrum needs warmth; spice it with clear coral, cream, olive green, bronze and palest yellow*

(Next spread right) *a grey backdrop comes to life with bright yellow, white, copper, ginger and burgundy*

deniers are for very extravagant moments). If you wear tights or stockings in summer with open-toed or sling-back shoes, they must be extra fine with sheer sandal heel and toe. Good quality tights and stockings are a small but essential expense to fit into a budget.

COLOUR-WISE

The **colour** of clothes in a small wardrobe is as important as the shapes. It makes sense not to limit the possibilities with a random colour scheme. The most workable wardrobe is based around a coordinated system where every garment has some link in colour as well as shape. The colour you choose is an entirely personal decision: be single-minded and wear what you love and only what suits you. Unlike fashion, colours never change, and there is no obligation to be in step with each season's 'right' shade. The most versatile approach is to use one neutral colour as a backdrop for everything else and build from there with related and contrasting colours.

Starting with a **basic colour** like navy, grey, beige or burgundy does not mean the whole wardrobe will revolve around dull unadventurous colours. Neutrals provide the perfect base for bright primaries, offbeat tones or delicate pastels. Each neutral has its own colour family where each colour enhances the others. Grey as a backdrop (every shade from pale silver to charcoal) works with ginger and rust shades, with scarlet, bright yellow, white and soft lilac tones. Navy works with grey, pale blue, dusty pink, white, cream and pale yellow. Burgundy (which needs to be a rich dark cherry shade) works with cream, gold, beige, pale pink, navy and cobalt blue. Beige is the hardest colour to bring alive: the danger is for the related tones to be too close together and murky which makes the colours look dead and unflattering. The best beige spectrum consists of clear clean shades of cream, khaki, olive green, chocolate brown, white, navy, bronze, coral and peach.

The danger with **colour planning** is to fall back on habit. It is easy to grow narrow-minded and stick with certain colours as a security. Some of the blame can be laid on sweeping generalizations which declare certain colours unsuitable for different hair types. Those old-fashioned rules presuppose that each hair colour has a standard skin colouring. Your hair colour, unless it is very extreme, is unlikely to clash with your clothes. It is skin tone that makes a colour look sensational on one blonde while doing nothing for another. It is worth trying on colours that you think are incompatible; they may well suit you.

Colouring combinations can only be very vague because everyone is so different. The pale skin that often goes with blonde hair and blue eyes

Navy, the most fool-proof basic colour, is enhanced by primrose yellow, dusty pink and essential touches of white and cream

needs warmth from a careful balance between soft colours which, if overdone, can look insipid, and dark strong colours which can drain colour from the face. The grey spectrum is particularly flattering for fair skin. Redheads often look good in the beige spectrum, with the emphasis on the peach and olive shades. If a skin tone is high (prone to red blushes) avoid hot colours like red, bright pink and ginger tones which accentuate the complexion. Some of the most flattering colours for every skin tone are shades of plum, claret and cherry red from the burgundy spectrum. Scarlet looks marvellous against medium and olive skin tones. It is strong without being overpowering, and much easier to wear than you might imagine. It is surprising how much colour can affect your mood. Some days you feel insignificant in neutral colours and need cheering up with a flash of something bright or luxurious. Maybe a shocking pink cardigan or a pair of primrose socks.

Certain combinations are guaranteed to look striking: navy and white, black and white, and navy, red and white. But there is also the danger of looking too predictable and over coordinated. The evenness of an outfit with white earrings and necklace, a navy shirt, white skirt, navy shoes, white bag, navy and white scarf is overdone. To avoid such a self-conscious balance, let one of the colours dominate or introduce an unexpected third colour: sand or olive green to navy and white, for example. With some experimenting, mixtures that were traditionally out of bounds, like green with blue, brown with black, brown with navy, pink with yellow or red, can be striking. Alternatively wear one colour. It has great impact providing you pick the right one. A total look in navy, light beige, black or cream is extremely elegant, but the same quantity in a bright yellow or hot pink is overpowering. Knowing where to draw the line is important. The quickest way to look overdone is to carry a strong colour through to all the accessories, especially tights. With a red dress and red shoes, sheer natural tights are more effective than sheer red ones. With thick or opaque tights, the density and bright colour become a definite part of the look, rather than a backup to the main colour.

A coordinated colour system does not exclude **patterned clothes**. A print is a clever way to introduce related colour and liven up plain separates. Prints are another matter of personal taste, but the most flexible designs are variations on stripes, checks, paisley themes and spots: classics that you can never tire of. Too many people have a mental block against mixing prints and textures. It requires skill and a good eye. It is not advisable to mix more than two different prints together and there must be a harmony between the designs; if they conflict the clothes look muddled. Learn how different stripes, or spots with stripes, can complement each other. As a guideline it is better to distinguish the different patterns in different materials. A softly striped cotton shirt with

Mixing prints is easiest and most effective if you keep to versatile unimposing patterns. Two unfailing classics together are stripes and a Madras plaid

There should be a harmony of colour and texture between each print. Paisley, tartan, checks and Fair Isle all blend successfully

a Fair Isle wool cardigan looks pretty, but a striped wool sweater under a Fair Isle cardigan looks a mess. When you mix two prints, it is best if the dominant one belongs to the more important garment. If you put a striped jacket over a check shirt, the stripes should be bolder than the checks. Mixing prints only really works with simple traditional patterns. Strong, fashion-inspired prints are less flexible; the design or motif becomes the focal point and overpowers the shape and style of the garment. There is nothing wrong with bold prints if you love the design and will not be tied by it, but it is not sensible to buy a mainstay garment in a print that has a limited appeal or versatility.

DRESSING YOUR FIGURE

Obviously the colours, prints and shapes you choose to wear are influenced by your figure type. If you have a large build, there is no reason to camouflage yourself in insignificant clothes, hoping that they will make you look smaller. Dress for your size, not to hide your body, but flatter it, even celebrate it, with the right colours and proportions. It helps if you understand how colour behaves on the body. In the same way that dark colours make you look smaller than light colours, hot colours – red, yellow, orange, yellow-based pink and ginger tones, all expand on a body, while cold colours – blue, green, purple, brown and grey, all contract. Since few figures are uniform, buying separates means you can find the right coloured and sized tops and bottoms. Avoid fitted shapes and go for clean lines in loose, but not baggy, separates. Watch the line where the garments meet: it becomes the most eyecatching area. Keep the colours in related tones instead of a stark contrast and avoid a glaring demarcation line. Unless you really want to show off a tiny waist, it should be defined, but not accentuated, with a loose narrow belt. One slimming illusion is to extend the colour of a skirt; if it is black, carry the colour through with sheer black tights and black court shoes. Other tricks are to hang your shoulder bag on a long, narrow strap, to wear a lightweight, narrow scarf instead of a bulky muffler; to restrict jewellery to long necklaces and simple, but bold, earrings.

If you are petite, you need to balance your clothes to your smaller frame. It is a mistake to wear fussy elaborate styles in place of simple shapes scaled down to your size. Avoid large prints which can swamp petite figures, and go for small, but never fiddly, patterns instead. Bypass high necklines and too many frills and ruffles. The most successful colour scheme revolves around warm, bright shades and pastels, especially cream, white and scarlet. Short legs can be elongated by keeping shoes and tights in the same colour tone. For accessories, choose small definite shapes; neat earrings and simple bangles.

It is rare to meet anyone who, given the chance, would not change the shape and size of at least one part of their body. The overdone concept of a 'perfect figure' turns those inevitable, usually inherited characteristics like a tiny or large bosom, a thick waist or broad hips, into major defects. You cannot change the basics of what you are born with. The only answer is to accept your body and learn how flattering the good points can divert attention from the not so good. The trick with wide hips is to play up your top half, and if you have one, to accentuate a small waist. Eye-catching ruffled, lacy or embroidered blouses, V-neck tops, sweaters and softly padded shoulders all draw the eye upwards. It is wise to avoid jackets, shirts or sweaters that come to the broadest curve of the hips. For a thick-waisted figure it is better to keep away from fitted clothes with waistlines. Instead, go for unstructured, generous shirts, smocks and sweaters that can be belted loosely into a low-waisted tunic shape. Again you need to draw the eye upwards with the help of light or bright colours and striking accessories – scarves, bold earrings or chunky necklaces. Keep away from gathered or drawstring skirts and draped bloomer trousers which enlarge the waistline. Bust sizes are a perpetual source of envy and dissatisfaction. Those who are well-endowed usually crave a smaller bosom, and vice versa. Small-busted figures can wear most shapes successfully, except for low-cut, off the shoulder or boned dresses that need a full bosom to carry them off and keep them up. With a large bust, what you wear depends on how much you want to emphasize. Anything very fitted or clinging, or jackets and shirts with bust-level detail like patch pockets, zips, bright stitching, all exaggerate the size and shape. The best minimizing lines are softly draped loose clothes; lean cardigan jackets with slim lapels, worn with narrow skirts or gently tapered trousers.

SHOPPING LOGIC

In spite of good intentions and logic, shopping expeditions can turn into frustrating ordeals. When you are in need of one specific thing, it is nowhere to be found, and when you browse with no intention of buying, you find something irresistible. Then there is the confrontation between heart and head. Despite the warnings from fashion pages, impulse buys often turn out to be successful because they are natural, instinctive buys. You are blinded by love for your find, which is the best possible motive to buy it. Even if you resist temptation at the first sighting, there seems to be a strange force that draws you back to the shop again.

If the object in question is not outrageously expensive and will belong in your wardrobe, there is little point in depriving yourself. It is better to buy clothes on that basis; all the fun goes out of shopping if you only buy from necessity. Some people like to buy their clothes in occasional sprees (often essential if you live away from a town), others prefer to shop at a slower pace and collect one thing at a time. The spree shopper needs to be strong-minded not to catch buying fever: it is easy to get carried away. If you buy one pair of shoes, why not have two? If you buy a new skirt, wouldn't it be fun to have something new to go with it? You let yourself be persuaded by an eager shop assistant to buy a top that may well go with the new skirt, but back home goes with nothing else. (The good shopper knows there are several things in her cupboard that will go with the new skirt, otherwise she would not buy it.)

There are disadvantages with a batch of new clothes. The novelty wears off at the same time and you need to avoid that rather clinical first-term, school-uniform look that a complete outfit of new clothes can have. They do lose the obvious freshly bought stamp when you mix them with established favourites from your wardrobe. Most new clothes take some wearing in before you feel at home in them and they look a part of you. If you can resist wearing all your new clothes the minute you buy them, it is worth keeping something back for a month or two. One new sweater can pep up a well-worn group of clothes.

The single-buy shopper needs a photographic memory of her wardrobe, so that every time she is tempted to buy, she knows how and where the new find will fit in. There are times when you find something that turns out to be invaluable, making you wonder how you ever managed before. It may be the simplest thing like a perfectly shaped bra, a great pair of jeans, shoes that are made for your feet or an irresistible lipstick or eye colour. If, when you discover the find, you can be convinced of its value it is definitely worth stocking up. It is exasperating to set your heart on an exact replica and find a month later that the shop has sold out, that the line has been discontinued or was a trial run in limited supply.

When the shops are full of a new season's clothes, it is a good idea to go on a shopping exercise with a notebook instead of a chequebook. The impact of many new possibilities can be bewildering and it is easy to make the mistake of buying something just to mark a new season, without being sure how much you like it. The best strategy is to browse through as many shops as possible, noting down the colours, shapes and prices you like, before buying anything. One rule is to try on everything, even tee shirts, unless you know and trust the brand. If you are looking for a skirt or trousers to go with a specific jacket, or vice versa, it is essential to take the jacket with you. When you buy something that is going to be a mainstay, take it on approval, if at all possible, to check how well it works with the rest of your clothes, and whether your opinion of it stays the same for twenty-four hours.

Shopping during sales times can be dangerous: few people are strong willed enough to ignore a bargain, and sales fever increases the temptation to buy something unnecessary because the price has been slashed. It is always worth considering the reason for such drastic reductions. Perhaps an original blouse or a pair of distinctively cut trousers are being virtually given away because they have hung, unbought and possibly unwearable, in the shop all summer long, or perhaps they are the last and least saleable of a disappearing fashion craze. It makes sense to invest in genuine reductions – quality articles like knitwear, leather shoes and bags, at a fraction of their original cost – providing the styles are simple. Sale pitfalls are high fashion or gimmicky clothes in unwearable colours; however smart the label, it is no reason to buy something you are not convinced about. It is wiser to buy more mundane essentials such as underwear, nightwear, socks and tights.

The timing of winter and summer sales does have advantages. Retailers keep half a season ahead of the buying public and fill their shops with summer dresses at the end of February and winter coats in August. If you have the patience to wait until December for winter clothes, and July for summer clothes, you can buy everything at sale prices. Obviously the cream of the stock is snapped up when it arrives at the start of the season, but the shops are forced to reduce the remaining clothes to make room for new deliveries. Before you invest in an expensive coat, find out when the sales start. Next week the same coat might be half price, and there is nothing more infuriating than someone else's bargain.

THE CLASSICS

Classic is a fashion term too often used to describe the kind of clothes that are not in the swing of high fashion. It is a definition of simple, low-profile dressing, but has unfair overtones of dull, rather prim clothes. The classics in this chapter are clothes that are fashion legends. They stand aside from the turbulence of high fashion with a timeless style. True classics last until they fall apart, rather than fall out of fashion.

So what makes a classic? The magic quality is a pure design with perfect proportions, free from any moods and extremes. Classics are completely natural and unimposing clothes for everyone to wear. As quality is a key point, these clothes may cost more than their counterparts, but they are investments that justify their price. Their style is not a uniform. There are classics in every type of dress: sporty, sophisticated, surplus, ethnic, country or jumble sale. Classic buying is a simplified approach to choosing fashion; it demands an instinct for the best colour, material and cut.

The vital point about a classic is **shape**. True classics have a permanent place in fashion because their shape can never be bettered; they are invaluable starting points for designers. Providing they do not stray far from the original, there are always beautiful classics to buy. The trouble starts when designers feel the need to add unnecessary detail to the basic shape. One of the best things about a classic is the way details and extras are pared down to an absolute minimum, so that every button, zip, seam, or pocket serves a purpose. Leading classics are legendary shapes that inspire copies at every price level. Top billing can be shared between the traditional Burberry-type trench coat, the plainest, small-collared man's shirt, the kilt, the Western jean, the twinset and the cardigan.

The 'British look' is made up of underrated classics which most people, except, it seems, the British, are keen to adopt. Every ingredient is a classic in itself: the traditional textures of tweed, tartan, fine cotton,

Classic fashion with timeless style

corduroy, flannel, sheepskin, Shetland, cashmere, Fair Isle and Argyll-checked knits, all in pure natural colours, worked into shapes which could not be less designed if they tried. Their potential tends to be overshadowed by their stuffy image, but take a lesson from cosmopolitan interpretations of the British style, which mixes such clothes with an essential dose of wit and originality. The bonus about the British look is that it is well interpreted at lower price levels. Each time it is reinstated from the borders to the centre of fashion, there is a crop of tweed coats, jackets, kilts, corduroy skirts and trousers, traditional knits and trench coats to suit different pockets, an opportunity for the discerning shopper to find the best quality and style for a low price.

Modern classics are the kind of basic clothes that have become indispensable. Blue jeans are a prime example. From being a symbol of anti-fashion, they have become a classic trouser. The need for much of fashion to be functional as well as decorative promotes casual sporty clothes into contemporary classics. A plain sweatshirt, a white tee shirt, a Fred Perry style tennis shirt, a tough leather motorbike jacket, dungarees, a tracksuit, khaki cotton trousers, are all modern classics.

Perfect tailoring: (right) *a fresh look at the most classic shapes*

(Bottom left) *easy country classics*

(Bottom right) *sophisticated town classics*

Those coveted British classics: (far left) *the Burberry trenchcoat, worn on the large side.*

In fine Scottish tradition (top left) *a timeless twinset and kilt. Key British textures* (bottom left) *sheepskin, suede and cashmere*

Hardworking classics: (right) *jeans jacket and dungarees*

*Classic versatility: the instant
rapport between an unlikely
mixture of contrasts; fragile silk
satin blouse under a casual suede
jacket, best straightlegged denim
jeans, shining lizard belt, bold
man's Rolex watch*

Surprise combinations:
(above left) *straw panama and tough tweeds with crisp white broderie anglaise*

(Above right) *chunky Aran knit over a soft tiered skirt*

(Right) *the flattering ease of a more generous cut*

How you wear the classics is as important as what you wear. Classic clothes have a neutral quality which does not impose on your character, so you have to take the initiative to create your own style from the perfect ingredients. Their charm is versatility, they look right in any place or situation. It is as if all the classics speak the same language and have an instant rapport with each other – even if one is an exquisite tailored shirt and the other is faded jeans, they still look good together.

To get the most from these clothes you have to see them from different angles. Develop unexpected combinations, create a surprise by mixing tough and soft clothes together, a thick ribbed sweater over a fine cotton skirt – or a tough leather jacket over a fragile silk camisole; by mixing old and new together, like an antique white lace blouse with sharp pinstripe trousers; by mixing formal and informal together – a cotton singlet with satin trousers, or a Shetland sweater flung over your shoulders with a silk dress. Try out certain things in a larger size than you would normally wear. A more generous cut, particularly with tailored jacket and shirts, relaxes the formality of the clothes and makes you feel more at ease and less 'dressed up'; and draped clothes are more flattering on the body than a tight fit. In the same way you can pull your clothes about until they feel

right and look a part of you – make the most of the little details like pushing up sleeves and turning back collars and cuffs.

Use colour to make the classics live. Detach yourself from what you expect and what others expect to see, and try to use colour with a fresh eye unchannelled by tradition or practicalities. Of course you should usually buy clothes in a sensible, versatile colour, but one that gives you pleasure each time you wear it. It is a surprise to find an established classic in an unexpected colour combination; a kilt in pastel tartan, pebbly Harris tweed in bright red or hunting green, a sheepskin coat in a crazy colour. Some combinations arc unbeatable, like blue denim, green loden, cashmere-coloured cashmere, grey flannel, white cotton. Others tend to go together out of habit. There is certainly no reason why raincoats always seem to be a depressing shade of beige or black.

THE FINER POINTS

What does a classic wardrobe include? There are no fixed rules, just flexible guidelines of shapes, colours, materials and patterns to follow. The material of the clothes is a critical point. There is something superior about natural fibres. They feel more comfortable to wear than man-made, they fall better, and most look good as they age. Synthetics tend to lose their original colour and texture, although a small addition of man-made to natural fibres *can* be undetectable, improve the wear and maintain the shape of the garment. The inferior synthetic image is vanishing while textile technology advances to produce replica silk, cotton and linen which look and feel natural enough, but have the advantages of being easier to wash, crease resistant and quick drying.

Pure wool is incomparable. It comes in such a range of textures that there is almost one suitable for every kind of clothing. Light woven weights like wool crepe, wool gaberdine, wool jersey and thin flannel are perfect materials for seasonless skirts, dresses and jackets. Tweed comes in a wealth of traditional and modern patterns, and a wide variety of thicknesses, some chunky enough for substantial overcoats, others fine enough for light trousers and tailored skirts. The most classic tweed patterns are the traditionals: hound's-tooth, herringbone, Prince of Wales, Harris fleck, Glen checks, Donegal speckles, all with a chameleon nature that makes them fit in with contrasting materials. A tweed jacket looks quite in place over a delicate lace blouse. And classic tweeds can go anywhere; the same jacket can look as good in the middle of a field as it does in the high street. Knitwear prices vary depending on the quality and type of wool. Luckily it is still possible to buy inexpensive pure wool knitwear, and as acrylic, the man-made alternative, lacks the

Herringbone tweeds that look marvellous in the middle of a town or a field

characteristic warmth and texture of wool it makes perfect sense to do so.

Cashmere is the ultimate in knitted luxury. It is the rarest natural fibre, combed from under the fleece of cashmere goats from Inner Mongolia. One sweater takes two fleeces, which proves how special and luxurious cashmere is, although the sheer joy of wearing it easily justifies the expense. The different grades and thicknesses (or plys) of cashmere are reflected in the price, which ranges from being expensive to quite out of the question for most people. The lowest priced cashmere sweaters which you may find in chain stores are not the most superior quality, but they are still well worth the investment. Pure cashmere does need special care because the fibres are so soft and fine. It is more resilient and cheaper when mixed with a percentage of lambswool. Shetland and lambswool have become general labels for two types of wool, and the top qualities of each can cost the same as cheap cashmere, but you can find both at surprisingly low prices. These do not feel quite as soft as the expensive brands, because they are knitted from medium- or low-grade fleeces, but they are still pure wool. The shaping of the sweater is often a criterion of its quality. It should be fully fashioned – knitted as a whole, with the sleeves properly set in, not sewn together from separate pieces. The best classic knitwear comes in the simplest old-fashioned stitches – cable, aran, ribbed and plain knitting – in solid colours, or the most classic Fair Isles, Argyll checks or pale intarsia rose patterns.

Leather and suede are examples of perfect classic materials that improve with age and are hardwearing; a quality that helps to justify their initial expense. But leather is not limited as an outdoor material. Fine suedes and leather can be as supple as light wool, and adapted into unstructured, simple shapes: easy drawstring trousers, wrap skirts, soft cardigan jackets, even shirts. The crucial point about suede and leather clothes is that the shape should be simple. They have a habit of accumulating unnecessary details – overdesigned touches, such as extra zips, stitching, contrast piping or a pretentious lining – which kill the charm of the material.

Silk is another quality fabric that tends to be treated as something wildly extravagant, but the wide choice of types, textures and cost of silk, make it as accessible, pricewise, as wool and cotton. The silk family includes crepe de Chine, satin, raw silk, organza, taffeta, chiffon, and various blends with wool or cotton. It is also remarkably strong and not as difficult to look after as some people imagine. Part of the charm of silk is the strong definition of colour, whether it is bright, pastel or muted. Unlike a synthetic equivalent, drab silk is hard to find.

Cotton is the cheapest of natural fibres. It is a beautifully comfortable fabric that comes in a wide range of woven and knitted textures; cotton lawn, voile, shirting, denim, mercerized, cellular, corduroy and velvet

Classic textures: Fair Isle knitting (top); silk crepe de Chine (above); workaday cottons, striped and checked (right)

are all definite classics. Most cottons are hard wearing, but it does pay to buy the best you can afford. Cheap corduroy, for example, tends to go bald and limp after several washes.

Denim must be the most well worn and famous version of cotton; it is certainly one of the most comfortable and cheapest materials (in terms of wear for money), and one that grows in style with age. A great pair of jeans depends on the quality and weight of the denim as much as the cut. The colour fastness and behaviour varies from brand to brand. If jeans are not preshrunk, they are likely to shrink about 8 per cent in the waist and leg. Sanforized denim means the jeans should shrink only 1 per cent. Indigo denim, which is dark blue, can be uncomfortably stiff at first, but softens and fades gradually with each wash. Pale blue, washed-out denim looks best in sunny countries, or chopped off as beach shorts; it still hasn't quite recovered from the strong links with frayed flares, slogans and patches. When denim is promoted sporadically from being a basic to an essential element of fashion, it becomes more than a pair of jeans, and features in skirts, shirts, dresses, jackets, hats, bikinis, shoes and bags, as well. When the designs of these denim fashions are pure and simple, they too rank as modern classics.

Denim: the utility classic. Wear Western jeans or the winning alternatives – a man-size jacket over white or checked cotton with the simplest skirt, a narrow button-through or little mini.

Summer denims – long-legged or cut-off dungarees over nothing but a suntan

But jeans outweigh the alternatives for guaranteed style. It is easier to look great in a pair of jeans, if you can find a pair to fit, than a jeans skirt. Jeans shopping is no more a question of Levis or Wranglers. The shops are swamped with different labels at different prices, all making claims to be the ultimate fit. At the top end there are designer jeans with a higher price that reflects the smart label on the pocket, more than a guaranteed superior fit. The problem with the middle-priced, traditional Western jean is that it suits a male shape better than a female one – cut for bodies with slim hips and no waist. Luckily the competitive market has spurred manufacturers to produce jeans that flatter a waist, fit round the hips and elongate female legs. Long skinny legs can take the cut of tapered jeans, but shorter legs look better with a high-waisted, straight jean. Once you find a shape that suits you, it is worth sticking to that brand. Jeans rank as a classic only if the styling is minimal and functional – after all they are the archetypal utility garment. They should be well constructed with double stitching on seams, pockets and flies, reinforcements on stress points (pocket corners, the zip base, belt loops), have a heavy-duty metal zip to last with the jeans, and at least five tough belt loops for a close fit at the waist.

SURPRISE CLASSICS

Another key point to classic style is the surprise of taking a traditional shape into an unexpected material. It is the same principle as switching colour combinations. You expect to find the classic jeans shape made up in denim, instead you find jeans made in silk or soft leather. Or take a man's singlet, a perfect natural shape, thought of as underwear or sportswear in knitted cotton, but with the twist of a different fabric like a chunky cotton knit, cashmere, silk jersey or linen, it turns into an individual classic. The same applies with tee shirts. The pure shape of a round or V-neck tee shirt translates perfectly into fabrics other than knitted cotton. The round-neck golfer cardigan, which you expect to see in knitted wool, adapts naturally into flannel, gaberdine, velvet, tee shirting, suede, and so changes from knitwear into a jacket.

Accessories are vital extras that add originality to classics. If ten fashion-conscious girls were given identical basic clothes to wear, but freedom with the accessories, each one would look totally different from the next. Their choice of shoes, belts, bag, socks, tights, jewellery, the mix of colours and textures all have a critical effect on the final appearance. For instance, the accessory permutations with one fine-checked cotton shirt are almost endless. It can be worn buttoned to the neck, decorated with a tie-pin brooch, a ribbon or bootlace bow tie, or it can be worn unbuttoned with a necklace or cotton kerchief. The sleeves can be rolled up to show off a loose steel watch, or two polished wooden bangles, or rolled down with bright cufflinks and a striped armband. The pocket might be discreetly monogrammed or contain a lace or spotted hankie. Each accessory has a character that influences the image of the shirt.

Accessories have to look like natural extensions of the clothes, not last-minute afterthoughts. With each outfit there is a perfect balance to gauge between the clothes and the accessories. Because classic clothes are essentially so simple, the danger is to feel underdressed and pile on too much of everything else to compensate. The result is a muddle with accessories competing against each other; it is much more striking to focus on one area. If a necklace is bold, there is no need for a belt with a dramatic buckle, and dangling earrings. Creating a focal point with your accessories is a subtle way to emphasize a particular part of your clothes. Use earrings to play up a collar, bracelets or rings for pretty cuffs, a necklace for a décolletage, or a belt to accentuate the texture of a sweater. Accessories tend to get pigeonholed into day and evening wear; casual, neutral colours and materials for day, glitter and vibrant colour at night, but this limits the scope of classic clothes. Everything has to be interchangeable – you *can* put a thick leather belt round a flimsy chiffon dress, and diamanté earrings with a sweat shirt.

Key accessories that influence the final image: stark black hat; Navajo silver and turquoise jewellery; men's braces; schoolgirl braided plaits

Belts are essential. A classic collection should include belts that are special enough to be the focal point of a look – perhaps a shiny bronze or brilliant suede sash, a cowboy belt in a delicious colour with a silver buckle – and belts that add an unobtrusive finish: simple narrow leather and suedes with square buckles, that work with all your clothes.

Scarves are such versatile accessories that they verge on being classed as clothes. Depending on the size and material, a scarf can be a winter shawl to wear instead of a coat (travel rugs also double as winter cloaks), it can be twisted into a bikini top, wrapped into a straight skirt or into a dress if sarong size. A scarf is an interesting way to add colour, introduce a pattern, or soften a severe neckline. It takes some experimenting in front of a mirror to tie a scarf that looks effortless – a studied knot or cravat with a scarf ring is too self-conscious. A silk square, unless large enough to drape nonchalantly round the shoulders, usually looks like a headscarf that has slipped from under the chin. Wool, cotton and lace scarves are easier to control than silk. Bright-coloured, checked and tartan mufflers or pastel cobweb mohair scarves can be twisted and knotted at the neck or in the hair. A large printed wool square folded into an oblong is an alternative to a knitted muffler. Plain, cotton squares add a surprise flash of summer colour, worn at the neck as a kerchief, or wound into a belt.

The idea of a classic **shoe** makes some people think of a sturdy lace-up brogue, or a Sloane Ranger slip-on trimmed with gold chains. But the classic definition applies to a shoe that is a perfectly simple design; a shape that is naturally flattering. Again the key is a lack of exaggeration or unnecessary detail: a heel that is not too unwearably high, spiky or wide; a toe that is neither too pointed nor square; straps that enhance the shape of the foot and line of the leg (thick ankle straps and elaborate lacing can make the legs look stumpy). From these guidelines, the most constant shoe shapes are the court shoe, the medium-heeled, slip-on mule, the moccasin or loafer, variations on the ballet pump, flat, lace-up walking shoes, which look better still if you change the laces for leather ones, and the riding boot.

When it comes to **jewellery**, there is a mental division that separates real and fake jewellery. There are no rules against mixing different kinds. Combinations of real, fake, ethnic or home-made, beads, earrings, necklaces and rings, can look highly original – especially worn in surprise circumstances; ethnic silver with a twinset, and delicate pearls with a leather jacket. Fake jewellery is fine, providing it is not blatantly plastic. The best fakes are the kind that can be mistaken for the real thing: pearls, coral, turquoise, amber, lapis, jet, jade, silver, gold, copper, brass, or diamanté impersonating diamonds. Otherwise choose inexpensive, natural materials like wood, tin, enamel, glass or sea shells.

A giant checked wrap to wear instead of a coat

OUTSIDE INSPIRATIONS

Fashion reflects the spirit of the day like a barometer, darting capriciously from one mood to another. It is affected by catalysts at different levels. The economic atmosphere plays a large part, with gloomy times inspiring nostalgic and escapist cults. The media have a more direct influence; films, television programmes, styles of art and pop music trigger off new and revival fashions.

The reaction to fashion influences has changed enormously since Hollywood days, when movie star styles and faces were idolized. Clara Bow personified the twenties flapper girl; Greta Garbo was adored for her elusive elegance and glossy page-boy hair; Joan Crawford prompted the craze for crimson, bow-tie mouths and square-shouldered clothes; Marlene Dietrich was worshipped for her cool sophistication and her sensational legs; the Veronica Lake vamp hairstyle covering half the face became a wartime factory hazard; Hedy Lamarr spread a wave of jet black hair after her starring role in *Samson and Delilah* and Marilyn Monroe's voluptuous figure was a symbol of glamour and female perfection. Other film stars have promoted specific fashions: Rita Hayworth popularized mannish forties suits with broad shoulders, nipped-in waists and straight skirts; Esther Williams, the champion swimmer who appeared in the 1944 film *Bathing Beauties*, gave new impetus to beach fashions; Lana Turner, the original 'sweater girl', boosted forties knitwear, and the large-scale imports of Italian knitwear in the fifties were attributed by some to admiration of Gina Lollobrigida. Brigitte Bardot with her admired vital statistics and air of knowing innocence brought fame to blue denim, pink and white gingham and broderie anglaise; Audrey Hepburn provided the contrast to the sex-kitten image and started the flat-chested gamine look in *Roman Holiday*, later echoed by Leslie Caron's French schoolgirl style in *Gigi*. The fashion explosion in the middle sixties was accelerated by Julie Christie as the heavy-lipped, mini-skirted model in the 1965 film *Darling*. Two years

Annie Hall dressing: a capricious mixture of anything old, borrowed and oversized

later, in *Bonnie and Clyde*, Faye Dunaway briefly reinstated the gangster beret and draped thirties knitwear. *Doctor Zhivago* prompted Russian-inspired fashions, and *Viva Maria*, helped by Brigitte Bardot and Jeanne Moreau, led to a brief Mexican-style revival of ruffles and flounces. *The Great Gatsby* brought back a feel for the twenties Jazz Age, with a sudden crop of Mia Farrow bobbed heads, slim wispy dresses with dropped waists and handkerchief hems, cloche hats and long beads.

Films in contemporary settings have epitomized the modern woman: in *Network*, Faye Dunaway played the prototype seventies career girl, whose ambitions were accentuated by her immaculately tailored boardroom suits and crisp silk shirts. The film *Annie Hall* actually invented a style that quickly became a widespread and permanent side to fashion. Diane Keaton, as Annie Hall, managed to turn unisex and women in men's clothes into something funny and relaxed, with a jumble-sale assortment of tweed jackets, baggy trousers, waistcoats, ties, hornrimmed spectacles and battered trilby.

Musical films often have a link with fashion by triggering off a period revival. The nostalgia boom for the fifties and sixties was helped along by college movies: *American Graffiti*, and later *Grease*, with Olivia Newton-John and her transformation to high school vamp in skintight black jeans and scoop neck top. Disco fashions were given a boost and widespread publicity by the ultimate disco movie, *Saturday Night Fever*, just as punk fashions were promoted by *Jubilee* and *Breaking Glass*.

Each musical cult has an influence on fashion – the clothes reflect what the music stands for. Rock-and-roll marked the beginning of a younger generation with their own style of music, fashion and idols. It meant full, swirly skirts, bobby socks, jaunty ponytails and dancing to Bill Haley and Elvis Presley. The revolutions of the swinging sixties, spurred on by Beatle music, brought brand-new fashions like the mini, kinky boots, tiny op art dresses – outrageous at the time, but full of fresh vitality. Fashion echoed the psychedelic phase in art and music with fantasy clothes in a kaleidoscope of dazzling colours and patterns. The Eastern influence that inspired hippies and the love and peace movement changed the music and brought a fashion for everything ethnic – afghan coats, peasant skirts, beads, caftans, Indian scarves and thonged sandals. Carnaby Street was quick to respond. Rock music has an image of heavy, black leather studded jackets, sloganed tee shirts and blue jeans. Punk was a temporary cult marked by aggressive music and similarly threat-ening clothes – ripped and zipped plastic and leather, bondage chains, safety-pin accessories, warrior make-up and spiky, multicoloured hair.

The follow-up to punk was labelled the 'new romantics'; a cult that spread further than the confines of a fashion-conscious elite, and infected every level of fashion. The look provided a perfectly timed escape from

Fashion influences:
(top row) *Greta Garbo, Joan Crawford;* (middle row) *Marilyn Monroe, Brigitte Bardot;* (bottom row) *Mia Farrow, Diane Keaton*

reality into fantasy; the clothes, having nothing in common with everyday life, were inspired by swashbuckling heroes, pirates, romantic warriors, highwaymen, and other Byronic romeos. At its most extreme, the look comprised huge ruffled smocks, slashed brocade jackets, pantaloons, admirals' hats, half-mast, cotton stockings, square-toed, buckled boots, tasselled sashes wrapped around the head, waist and hips, hair in tiny plaits, faces painted with freckles and dusted with gold powder, eyes and lips outlined in black. The seeds of the piratical style grew, like so many other fashion cults, from Vivienne Westwood and Malcolm Mclaren's fashion Mecca which they have renamed (for the moment) 'World's End'. The Kings Road shop has housed the extremes of each musical/fashion lead. In 1971 it was 'Let It Rock', selling Teddy Boy clothes; in 1972 it became 'Too Fast To Live Too Young To Die', and sold rockers' motorbiking leathers; in 1974 it changed to 'Sex', and pioneered rubber and leather prepunk uniform. In 1977 it turned into 'Seditionaries', the original punk HQ. Now 'World's End' is pure Errol

Roller Disco: a craze that prompted its own fashion

Cult uniform from World's End: the 'new romantics' in full swaggering rig

Flynn and Captain Blood. At the first pirate fashion show in March 1981, Malcolm McLaren's band Bow Wow Wow pumped out, off the beat, the words, T-e-k- Technology! A-u-t- Autonomy! as the romantic heroes and heroines gyrated through a haze of gunpowder cloud and applause. The programme manifesto read, 'cassette pack on your back, loin cloth between your legs, gold braid in your hair, a modern day pirate: you use technology as pirates used to use their slaves, and it works for you'.

The disco scene coincided originally with the arrival of the American health kick. Fitness became an obsession and disco dancing provided perfect calorie-burning, muscle-toning exercise. In the heat of the craze, the disco look influenced the shape, colour and texture of fashion. Clothes grew like second skins in shiny stretch fabrics, as bright and as iridescent as possible. The leotard really came into its element, worn on its own as an 'all-in-one', or with satin boxer shorts and footless tights. The boob tube in Lycra or stretchy sequins was a party favourite for those who could dance and keep it up at the same time. One step on was roller-disco, which started the fashion for mini skating dresses and skirts in vibrant disco colours. Running parallel with the disco look was the sportswear look. Fitness is almost a vicious fashion circle. Disco clothes only look good on a well-exercised body, so before people took to the dance floor, they took up jogging and other athletic pursuits, which inevitably demanded a fashion of their own. Tracksuits, running shorts and sweatshirts emerged quickly in unsporting bright and pastel colours and new velour materials, intended for more than work-outs.

The whole health kick has had an influence on our attitude to fashion. The unbelievable comfort and ease of sportswear has made new demands on the shape of contemporary fashion. Now the shape of the body rules the shape of fashion; clothes show off a well-exercised body, they no longer disguise or contort it. The influence is double sided – you cannot look good in sportswear-based fashion unless you have the figure for it. The simple, unstructured fashions need to be worn over a healthy body; not necessarily skinny, just very fit. The contemporary heroine might model herself on the energy and athletic prowess of Charlie's Angels, Bo Derek or Wonder Woman.

FASHION ROOTS

Ethnic inspiration: Kenzo's multicoloured peasant look

While these cults have a varied and transient effect on fashion, the inspiration that comes from national dress is constant. Many of the shapes, patterns and colour mixes that recur are based on the traditional designs of different national costumes. The styles survive the passing of time because they are deeply rooted in the origins of their country, based

on timelessly simple and practical shapes and made from naturally available materials, coloured and patterned to reflect the environment. National costume is a rich source of fashion in its purest sense. Taken too literally it becomes fancy dress – no one needs to dress up as a bona fide Hungarian folk dancer, or an Indian squaw in full war paint – but there is a wealth of tradition that can be borrowed and translated into contemporary fashion.

Too often, designers have to take the lead and show a Russian- or Oriental-inspired collection before anyone is brave enough to experiment with or see the potential in any authentic clothes they may be hoarding – the ethnic souvenirs you buy and wear on holiday that feel out of place back home. Ingenious designers cast new light on national costume by giving it modern treatment. They juggle the pieces unexpectedly; adjust the proportions slightly, add some contemporary details, rethink the colours, yet retain the hallmarks that give it a definitely Mexican, Chinese, jungle, or wherever look. When the clothes of a particular nationality come into fashion, there is an inevitable epidemic of ethnic imitations in the shops. These mass-produced versions (unless they spring from the country of origin) often lack the charm of the genuine

article because the traits that characterize the style are scaled down for commercial success. Obviously the actual designer clothes that spark off each ethnic look are desirable because they are originals in their own right. After all, who would say no to a genuine Kenzo peasant dress, or Saint Laurent matador? But the authentic thing, besides being much cheaper than a designer label, does have winning qualities. It is the look in its purest form, without the fickle lifespan of anything stamped by fashion.

Historical and contemporary dress from the Orient has had an enormous influence on fashion. The perfect simple shapes, the rich colours and traditional prints, the sumptuous embroideries and materials tempt designers to take their inspiration from the East. Collections with a Chinese or Japanese feeling invariably reflect the native cultures: Chinese dragon prints; Ming porcelain colours; lotus blossom designs that contrast with swashbuckling Samurai warrior styles. The kimono influences the cut of contemporary coats, jackets, cardigans, blouses and dresses. Its soft, unconstructed lines epitomize the freedom that belongs with the most wearable modern fashion; an easy wrap instead of zips or buttons. An obi sash, the traditional kimono belt, reappears as a key accessory in Oriental collections.

Other characteristic shapes are the mandarin jacket: slim, single breasted with a small stand-up 'Mao' collar; the cheongsam, a narrow, asymmetrically fastened tunic, often worn over wide-legged drawstring silk or cotton coolie pants. Quilted and padded clothes come from the Orient, and have been interpreted to form a permanent and practical side of fashion.

Besides the inspiration from the basic shapes and textures of Asia, the genuine articles are definitely worth investigating. Shops with Oriental stock are full of surprisingly inexpensive finds. Look out for embroidered silk or cotton pyjamas, smart enough to wear in the evening with beaded velvet Chinese slippers, or fine silk embroidered petticoats to wear as sundresses. Cotton kimonos make useful dressing gowns, but they also adapt into summer wrap dresses or beach robes.

Another Eastern influence on fashion is the recurrent feeling for peasant clothes that stems from regions like Mongolia, Tibet and South America. They inspire cold weather clothes in layers of mixed patterns and textures: sheepskins, alpaca, blanket shawls, woollen dirndl or tiered long skirts, homespun knits, flat suede or leather boots, thick ribbed leggings, headsquares under bowlers and Davy Crockett hats, all in a random jumble of vivid stripes, paisleys, florals, plaids and checks, coloured with the richness of a brilliant tapestry. Peru is a great source of peasant knitwear, renowned for the distinctive Inca sweaters in garish green, pink, yellow, turquoise combinations, decorated with stripes and paperchain cut-outs; and the more sombre brown and cream alpaca knits patterned with primitive Aztec and animal motifs. The appeal of these sweaters is the texture and colouring which is not easy to imitate. Machine versions tend to be wishy-washy and too uniformly designed.

The most accessible ethnic fashions come from India. Too many people still associate Indian fashion with shapeless hippy dresses hung with bells and long drooping scarves, dismissing anything Indian as part of the musky past. But now Indian clothes have much in their favour. They are well priced, mostly well made in pure cotton or silk, richly coloured, finely patterned and embroidered, and limited to simple shapes. Traditional Indian colours reflect the country – hot curry colours, strong spicy shades of cinnamon and paprika woven into madras-checked cottons, some threaded with glints of silver or gold. The most striking Indian silks are vivid shades of peacock blue, magenta and flame red. For best effect, the clothes need to be mixed with Western classics. The uncrushable crinkly cotton skirts look good with plain tee shirts and sweaters, and an intricate embroidered Indian blouse looks best with a simple pair of jeans or plain skirt. The long printed silk and cotton scarves make versatile accessories; they knot round the neck several times, twist into belts, turbans, headbands or wind into a colourful bandeau bikini top. When saris are unravelled they stretch for yards, but a child-size one can be worn as an exotic evening wrap, or as a diagonal sash knotted at

Colonial Zouaves from the Indian Raj by Armani, Versace and Perry Ellis

Indian Nehru fashion: essential white hat, little black shades, wide cotton layers and neat feet

The Fair Isle tradition (opposite) *hand knits in soft Scottish colours*

(Next spread right) *in the jungle with Kenzo's native cottons*

Russia's peasant colours (next spread left) *one Saint Laurent blouse among the ethnic brilliance*

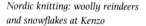

Nordic knitting: woolly reindeers and snowflakes at Kenzo

the hip. Indian-inspired zouaves, or harem pants, are an addictively comfortable trouser shape – basically a draped bloomer gathered from the waist and falling in folds of cotton or silk to the knee, mid or low calf. They look marvellous in summer worn with bare legs, flat leather sandals and a soft shirt or simple cotton sweater. The essential point with zouaves is to emphasize the waist, or they can look unflatteringly bulky. Indian history has left its mark on two recurrent fashion shapes. Jodhpurs take their name from the state of Jodhpur, and the Nehru jacket and hat, cropped, single-breasted, little white coats and small flattened chef's hats, were inspired by the first post-Independence prime minister, Nehru. Madras is a perennial fashion fabric, traditionally hand-woven, vegetable-dyed cotton, produced only in Madras.

Some of the crispest cottons come from Mexico. Their starchiness inspires voluminous skirts, dresses, puff-sleeve blouses, nightdresses, wedding dresses, with rows of fine pintucking, lace panels and ruffles. In white, the clothes are the nearest contemporary fashion to antique white lace, but in the characteristic stark black, scarlet, turquoise and magenta, they are strongly Mexican and can be just as dramatic. The poncho is a sadly over-exploited Mexican garment. The original square, striped blanket with a hole cut out for the head has been horribly sophisticated into fringed tweedy capes, and should definitely be bypassed.

Closely related to a Mexican style is the South American Carmen Miranda look, a Spanish influence that inspires cleavage dresses with tightly corseted bodices, off-the-shoulder frills and graduated frothy skirts – clothes to suit a seductive *femme fatale*. The gipsy look is similar, but less contrived. A bohemian mixture of exotic colours and random layers, characterized by gold hoop earrings and a headscarf knotted under Romany curls.

Ethnic knitwear is a constant influence on fashion. The Nordic theme inspires chunky sweaters dotted with snowflakes, reindeer and Arctic variations. The traditional colouring is navy and white, but some of the most original adaptations come in iced pastels. The influence from Irish knits is in the texture – knubbly mixes of blackberry and diamond shapes in thick, creamy wool which translate perfectly into short, cotton knits in every colour. Fair Isle patterns are the most classic ethnic knit, and as a result are probably the most copied on a commercial scale. Because it is such a traditional style, even the mass-produced Fair Isles have a certain appeal, but they seldom have the old-fashioned blend of muted colours that distinguishes a genuine Scottish Fair Isle from the copies. Nostalgia for traditional sweaters has revived the knitted-by-Granny look, particularly anything reminiscent of a thirties or forties handknit. Unless you have an industrious granny, these handknits are prohibitively

expensive because each one is unique. The cheapest answer is to invest in a sleeveless sweater which works over everything, or on its own, day and night. If you are a knitter, look out for back copies of women's magazines. Amongst the recipes and romances you may come across some covetable contemporary-looking forties-style knitting patterns.

The kilt must be one of the most fashion-orientated pieces of national dress. It never goes out of fashion, but comes into its element when designers produce collections with a Highland theme – accompanied by a rush of tartan and plaid shawls, sashes, mufflers, tam o' shanters and white, high-neck frilly blouses. It is a look to take up in moderation, as a surfeit of sashes and sporrans looks like a Highland reeler in full rig. Scottish dressing requires individuality. A genuine kilt is a wonderful classic, but needs relaxing with non-Scottish, feminine coloured knitwear and informally ruffled shirts. Kilts can look original worn above the knee with bright coloured thick tights and flat loafers. It is difficult and almost criminal to cut off a hem, so it is worth investigating children's departments for junior sizes in short lengths.

The folkloric influence is another inspiration; loosely based around fairy tales and children's book pictures of Hansel and Gretel characters in immaculate Tyrolean walking outfits. Lederhosen and braces apart, the fashion pointers are embroidered, white cotton drawstring blouses, appliquéd boleros, circular felt skirts with decorated borders, feathered Tyrolean hats, and cropped, forest green or scarlet jackets edged with braid and silver buttons.

The Russian influence is also based on folklore and the arts. Russian peasant fashions are reminiscent of the traditional wooden mama dolls, painted with brilliant flowery headscarves and multi-striped skirts, petticoats and long aprons. The voluminous cossack style stems from Tolstoy heroines. Anna Karenina silhouettes of dramatic black cloaks, braided, fitted velvet coats with swirling skirts, over high-buttoned lace blouses, with fur toque hats, deep fur muffs, cossack boots – all reflecting the romantic wintry associations of Russia. Colours are usually rich and sombre; mainly black, wine, bottle green and dark navy in a sweeping mix of fur, thick wool, velvet, brocade and lace. The Oriental costumes of Diaghilev's Ballet Russe still inspire modern fashion. The Arabian Nights theme of *Scheherezade*, the most visually exotic ballet, is a literally fantastic source of rich colours, textures and patterns. It recalls sumptuous fabrics, billowing shapes of harem pants, draped sparkling turbans, embroidered, bejewelled jackets, in a brilliant spectrum of gold, emerald, cobalt blue, turquoise, flame and silver.

The jungle look, influenced by dreams of tropical paradise and Crusoe-ish desert islands is a recurrent theme for hot weather dressing, inspiring scanty, mostly cotton clothes, decorated with exotic wild life, birds of

Folk-lore style (previous spread left) *Fendi's full-skirted coat with Highland wrap and Argyll leggings*

Mexican cottons: (previous spread, right) *a traditional embroidered nightdress worn loosely belted as a summer smock*

(Opposite) *Kenzo's Cossack style in sweeping brown leathers*

paradise, palm trees, tropical fruit, sun, sea, animal markings and tribal prints. There are two sides to jungle fashion: the tarzan style, or the white hunter style. The tarzan look is minimal and comes in hot sunshine colours; brief bikinis and swimsuits, one-shoulder tops, vests, and the most essential kanga – a multipurpose, batik type printed cotton rectangle that can be a sundress, a skirt, a belt, a scarf or a sunbathing mat. Authentic kangas or sarongs from Africa or Bali are the most covetable, but you can improvise with a large cotton oblong. The white hunter look is suitable for cooler climates. Key points are safari, knee-length shorts, a crisp cotton shirt, a very simple safari jacket and a white hunter's hat with a mosquito net veil, all in neutral desert tones of sand, buff, khaki, white and eau de nil. Ethnic accessories are an important part of each look. Jewellery should be bold and primitively shaped: handmade necklaces, chokers, worry beads, wide carved bangles and earrings made from natural resources like wood, shell, bone or sharks teeth. The best jungle belts are in tough brown leather, sashed gold kid or printed cotton. Footwear should be flat and practical: thonged leather sandals, espadrilles or canvas pumps worn with bare legs or white ankle socks.

Cowboy clothes are more than an influence, they belong as a part of fashion – practical, knockabout, sexy clothes that look just as good on urban cowgirls as they do back West. The main ingredients are well-worn, straight-leg jeans, mansize wool or cotton check shirts, silver-buckled, tooled, leather cowboy belts, cuban-heeled cowboy boots to go under, not over, the jeans. Optional extras: a denim jean jacket, classic sheepskin coat or waistcoat, a jeans skirt, preferably mini, a genuine or toyshop stetson, red and white spotty handkerchiefs to fold into triangular kerchiefs, silver buffalo 'bolo' ties, leather bootlaces to tie in the hair or keep up the sleeves of an eagle-printed shirt. If the whole Western look seems too overpowering, the trick is to soften the cowboy clothes with some surprise feminine touches. Substitute the check shirt for an embroidered silk one, or a pastel Shetland; wear a lace scarf instead of the kerchief; swop denim jeans for pink corduroy, and regulation tan cowboy boots for a bright red pair.

The Red Indian tradition has also inspired fashion. Cowboys and Indians are often grouped together, and the influence that should be attributed to Red Indians is usually overlooked and referred to as part of the Western style. The Indian look is characterized by Hiawatha-style headbands, fringed shirts, tunics, trousers and skirts in pale chamois. The accessories are distinctively Indian, especially the silver and turquoise Navajo jewellery, the finely beaded leather belts and the archetypal white leather Indian moccasin.

Frontier fashion: a cross between the cowgirl and Red Indian tradition. The Wild West spirit inspires broderie anglaise blouses and petticoats, woollen jackets, trailing prairie skirts and pioneer boots

THE ALTERNATIVES

One of the most irritating points about wearing clothes from inexpensive chain stores and boutiques is the chance of meeting someone else dressed identically. Being confronted by a mirror image at a party or in the street can take all the pleasure out of your new clothes. A solution is to find your wardrobe from alternative places. In every town, however quiet it may appear, there is disguised fashion potential. Untapped, original treasures wait to be exploited by an adventurous and imaginative shopper in local jumble sales, thrift shops, antique markets, sports shops, traditional men's outfitters, children's departments and government surplus stores. Finding clothes in these alternative sources is a time-consuming business. You need patience and perseverance to explore every possibility, to scrutinize the shop stock (probably exasperate the proprietor), and try on anything that looks promising. When you do find something to buy, the thrill of an original bargain is immeasurably satisfying. Alternative shopping can become addictive. Like collecting old books or junk china, you develop a craving to check out every shop in each new town you visit, anxious not to bypass any treasure.

To make a success of this style and avoid looking like an over-dressed magpie, you need a well-tuned eye and a talent to sift the genuine finds from the rubbish. How you wear the clothes counts as much as what you wear. You need the skill to make something extraordinary look intended and not like fancy dress, the flair to mix old, new and contrasting styles together – call it 'cross-dressing'. It is a fresh way of seeing clothes requiring elastic economic values. For instance your scarf may cost more than your entire outfit, but it might be just what you need to add polish to the look: you should never overpay for second-hand clothes, especially ones in poor condition, but before you reject your find for being too expensive, it is worth considering how much the modern chain-store equivalent would cost instead. Second-hand (especially men's) clothes

How you wear the clothes counts as much as what you wear. You need the skill to make something extraordinary look intended, not like fancy dress

need working at before they start to look good. As well as having them immaculately reconditioned, ironed and starched you need ingenuity to spot new ways of wearing traditional clothes – to turn them back to front and inside out, to hitch men's trousers to skim the ankle or chop them off at the knee. It is essential to treat the style with a sense of humour and spontaneity. The minute you start to take it all too seriously, it becomes pretentious.

BARGAIN TACTICS

Buying second-hand clothes has turned into a cult. As the passion for nostalgia increases, the second-hand market is swamped with a mass of old clothes, many of which are vastly overpriced, tatty and without charm. The quantity of second-hand clothes available, whether in jumble sales, fêtes, bazaars, auctions or markets, is an incentive in itself to track down anything worthwhile. But it is easy to get carried away by the bargain atmosphere: unless you have enough space to keep a private junk shop, it is important to keep ruthlessly high standards.

At the top end of the second-hand clothes market, prices seem to soar out of proportion because the clothes are limited and much in demand. The clearest example is the fashion for Victorian white lace clothes. Each time the antique look is revived, the clothes double or treble in price. The shrewd alternative shopper buys her Victorian lace before the market reacts to the boom. Shops in London and major cities are always quick to realize the potential profits, but as is often the case with old clothes, some wonderful bargains can still be found in towns around the country, away from the pulse of fashion. Shops to head for are the sort that sell a mixture of junk and bric-a-brac and a few clothes suspended from picture hooks, draped over decaying statues, or tucked away negligently in a corner. Country markets often have stalls selling old clothes which are definitely worth investigating. Local house sales occasionally include an assortment of clothes, although anything special seems to be snapped up by eagle-eyed dealers and collectors for a staggering price.

Unless it really *does* only cost twenty pence, it is a mistake to buy anything from a second-hand store in a hurry. Making friends with the shopkeepers can be very rewarding; they may unearth some hidden prize stock for you to see, and respond to a spot of bargaining – which is always worth a try. (Never make remarks about the low prices, they will have doubled by your next visit.) Before you buy, examine every garment in daylight for moth holes, tears, stains and faded patches. If any buttons are missing, see if the shop sells anything similar, otherwise find unobtrusive bone or mother-of-pearl buttons in a haberdashery

It is essential to treat the style with a sense of humour and spontaneity. The minute you take it too seriously, it becomes pretentious

department. If they are intact, it is worth resewing them all securely. Be realistic about how much repair is needed before the garment will be wearable. If it has already been mended in several places, the material will be weakened and might not stand up to further work. Even if you cannot sew, it helps to understand alterations; which changes are straightforward, which are more involved and expensive. Replacing zips, mending broken seams and torn linings are fairly simple jobs, and depending on the material and existing hem, most garments can be altered in length or taken in. Removing shoulder pads from coats and jackets can turn into a complicated structural alteration, best left to a professional, as it involves taking out the lining as well. If the lining is not replaced, the garment often loses its original shape and looks droopy.

As a general rule it is not worth buying something second-hand with the idea of totally reshaping it. In most cases you have to take it as it is. But should you find a large-sized bargain coat, jacket or suit in a beautiful, well-preserved material, find an inexpensive tailor to scale it down for you. It is pointless to buy anything badly stained that is too fragile to stand up to washing or dry-cleaning. Fortunately most natural fibres keep their resilience and can be restored. Silk is the weakest natural fibre and there are mixed opinions about cleaning. It is less of a risk to dry-clean delicate silk, providing you check with the cleaners which chemicals they use. Cotton and linen are much tougher and have more chance of being completely reconditioned. White cottons can be boiled up with bleach in a saucepan, or left to soak in a cold water solution. Rust marks spoil the look of white cottons, and can be prevented by removing the hooks, eyes and any other metal fastenings before the cleaning process starts. Existing stains can be rubbed before a wash with the old wives' remedy of half a lemon dipped in salt.

Fortunately there is still a wide selection of Victorian and Edwardian white lace in nearly mint condition, well-preserved in their time under layers of outer garments, hidden from heavy wear and tear. What was originally intended as underwear now adapts beautifully into everyday clothes. The antique cotton and lace petticoats make perfect skirts; when one is too transparent, if you can afford another, wear two together, one longer than the other. A white lace blouse is the most attractive item of antique clothing because it is so extraordinarily versatile. It works with every single style, shape and texture, from a plain Shetland jersey, a tough tweed or thick leather jacket to sequins, velvet, sheepskin, suede or more white lace. Fragile cotton camisoles with little buttons or a ribbon drawstring make pretty summer tops. Antique white cotton nightshirts with ruffled lace collar and cuffs can be worn as dresses or cut off into billowy shirts. White cotton pantaloons make fine summer bloomers, belted with thick leather or a bright scarf. Lace fichus, lace collars and

An antique cotton and lace chemise; once strictly underwear, now a most covetable top layer

even antique lace runners intended for dressing tables all make exquisite scarves, belts or hair bands. However much of it all you choose to wear, the finish is critical. Everything does need to be well laundered and crisply starched, chipped or missing buttons replaced, frayed ribbons mended or renewed. Of course it doesn't *have* to be white. If the material is stained or blotchy you can dip it in a solution of weak tea to make it a soft biscuit colour.

CLASSIC TREASURES

There are certain nostalgic classics that are worth snapping up. For example, in knitwear: thirties and forties originals, little cardigans and puff-sleeved fitted sweaters in faded Fair Isle designs or lacy stitches; any hand knits, particularly more Fair Isle type patterns on men's V-neck slipovers; soft wool classic beaded cardigans, which vary in price depending on the state of the beading and moth holes; sorbet-coloured fifties mohair sloppy sweaters. Other treasures are American bowling shirts, with the home team emblazoned across the back; embroidered silk camisoles or blouses; antique ethnic embroideries; quilted satin jackets, or brilliant silk kimonos. You can find classic tweed coats and jackets that may be twenty or thirty years old, but still look contemporary. Men's tailored jackets often improve with age; there has been enough time for the rigidity to be worn away, leaving a soft movable jacket, supple enough to roll the sleeves up and belt like a cardigan. The epitome of the antique market look is the Granny tea dress in printed crepe or rayon; waisted, with a neat lace collar and elbow-length cuffed sleeves. The evening find, rare now, is a flapper style beaded or sequinned Gatsby dress, complete with a beaded headband, long cigarette holder and fur boa. Jumble fur coats are not usually worth buying, unless you need to be warm and nothing else. Most look rather mangy and dilapidated. If you do find a passable one, it looks best worn in the evening when the light is kinder. Second-hand shops are a great source of original accessories. Antique costume jewellery is satisfyingly indeterminate because no one ever knows how much you paid for it, or whether it is a real family heirloom. Accessible finds are imitation or real black jet, coloured glass beads, drop earrings like chandeliers, diamanté paste brooches, neck-laces and tiaras, cameo brooches, stick pins and hat pins. Look out for rarities such as tapestried carpet bags, embroidered silk evening purses on long gilt chains, lace handkerchiefs, fans and long kid button gloves, to carry if you cannot fit into them.

SURPLUS STYLE

Surplus bargains: (top) *khaki Boy Scout's shirt with army fatigues;* (below) *blue cotton Girl Guide's dress*

Another great source of bargains is the government surplus store. But the style does need careful treatment to step out of the uniform mould and be feminized. Treat surplus clothes as separates, isolate individual garments and mix them with contrasting, particularly feminine things. Although khaki is not flattering against pale skin, it looks marvellous with plenty of other colours; anything pastel, primrose, lilac, pale blue, cream, white. The trick is to avoid other drab colours, or shades too close to a khaki tone. And a pair of army shorts somehow looks far more glamorous than their £1 price tag implies if you wear them with your best belt and a good shirt.

One of the quandaries of buying surplus clothes is not knowing which size to take. It is impossible to make rules, as so much depends on how you look in a particular garment; whether you want to flaunt your figure in tight shorts or boilersuit, or camouflage it under folds of material. But clothes that are too enormous will swamp you, which is not the point of wearing the clothes. You do not actually want to look as if you belong in the army or work as a plumber's mate. You wear the clothes because they are cheap, but also because they are simple enough to be transformed into an individual style.

Army surplus classics are knee-length white or khaki cotton drill shorts which look good with a white tee shirt, or even a white lace shirt, bare legs and flat gold sandals. Mansize shorts are fine as long as you define the waist with a belt and keep your top half fitted. If the shorts are too long, try rolling the legs up to mid-thigh level. A long jacket over shorts looks out of proportion and very unflattering from behind. Depending on the stock in your surplus store, you may find thick, cotton, padded combat jackets. They are waterproof, windproof and make great everyday jackets. The US Army issue comes in an attractive buff colour, which makes a change from khaki. Woollen army shirts are a perfect classic shape, with small pointed collars, breast pockets and long shirt tails but they are often too prickly to wear next to the skin, so can be turned into light-weight jackets to go over tee shirts or thin sweaters. The standard white or service blue collarless shirts make surprise mini dresses, or useful nightshirts, especially as they are often the cheapest things in the store. The accessories are worth exploring – amongst the first-aid kits and torches, hunt for knitted pull-on beenie hats, leather-edged berets, towelling or wool comforter scarves, canvas satchel bags, webbing belts and woolly socks.

Each time the nautical look is fashionable, bargain hunters dive to the nearest surplus store for the real thing. If you can find them, white and navy sailor tops look best worn like short smocks, over white drill sailor

Army surplus classics: keep the look surprisingly feminine and wear flounced silk, lace or cotton with your khaki shorts, canvas belt, penknife and rucksack

Key surplus proportions: keep it neat and fitting from the waist up, with wide cinched belts, cropped jackets and remember to check the look from behind . . .

trousers. The thinner, white cotton naval jackets are more successfully adapted than winter issue navy blue ones which tend to look too theatrical. Navy sailor boat-neck sweaters are incredibly warm and partially waterproof, they look less bulky than Guernseys at a fraction of the price. Rifle through collections of old buttons and trimmings; if a shirt or jacket is going cheap, it may be worth it just for these. Other sea-faring bargains can be found in sailing shops. Amongst the compasses and logbooks there is a store of proper nautical fashion. Look for traditional yellow oilskins and sou'westers, white and blue matelot tee shirts, Breton sailing jerseys, in striped or plain navy, red and cream, always with the characteristic three buttons down the shoulder. There are thick, oiled sweaters in warm tweedy wool, smarter navy knitted cardigan jackets (meant for the yacht club, but perfect with jeans). The best of these shops are filled with random extras which make great accessories; polka-dot handkerchiefs, silver whistles on chains, bright parachute nylon holdalls, thick socks, woolly hats, peaked captain's caps in navy felt or white cotton.

Not all uniform clothing comes from the armed services. There is a wealth of surplus bargains intended for waiters, chefs, plumbers and workmen that can be bought brand new from civil service or trade stores. All the clothes are wonderfully cheap, but as function is a more important criterion than style, they usually need to be dressed up imaginatively. Uniforms to investigate are white cotton drill boilersuits, to wear belted with the sleeves and legs rolled up; white or navy cotton drill dungarees, worn large and belted over a tee shirt or sweatshirt; button-fly blue and white check cotton chefs' trousers, to wear long, or cut off as Bermuda shorts; white cotton waiters' jackets with slim lapels or a curved shawl collar, which can be dyed to a bright colour; and for winter, navy wool workmen's jackets – the best have leather patches across the shoulders.

STYLE IN THE BEST TRADITION

School uniform departments are worth browsing through. Boys' tweed jackets or unlined flannel blazers in grey, navy or bottle green are inexpensive and completely classic buys (if you don't object to buttoning on the boy's side). Sports jerseys are often original and good value, especially pure wool, cream, cable cricket sweaters and slipovers, or thick football sweaters with little collars. Regulation school knitwear can also be a classic find; look out for plain, ribbed V-necks with the school stripe around the neck and cuffs. Several designers have rediscovered divided games skirts, so economize with the genuine article; the winter

(Above) *checked chef's trousers*

(Left) *seamanship: head-to-foot nautical kit from sailing stores*

'Boy's Own' style: the best
pickings from traditional
menswear counters, school
uniform departments, surplus
stores and jumble sales. Look out
for collarless shirts, worn neat
with a stud; boy's pyjama tops to
go under Fair Isle or cabled vests
and waistcoats; wide tweedy
trousers, held up by braces or a
paisley cravat slotted through the
belt loops. On the feet: shiny
leather lace-ups and Argyll socks

netball flannels with bright warm tights and flat shoes, the navy cottons with bare legs, painted toenails and strappy sandals. The most covetable school accessories are stretchy boys' snake belts and brown leather or canvas satchels, which make extremely practical handbags.

Men's departments, or the traditional male outfitters, can be havens of alternative fashion. Top priority is to charm the salesmen. Gentlemen's shops are still bastions of masculinity and may not welcome or see the funny side of a tiresomely thorough female shopper. You may have to accept rather condescending service, but don't be deterred. Some of the more desirable articles of men's clothing are the most conservative classics: quietly checked Viyella shirts, discreet, striped Oxford cottons with button-down collars, the collarless striped shirts that go with stiff collars, pie-frilled or pintucked white cotton dress shirts, collarless if possible. The best men's knitwear is the simplest, with no trace of fashion design, except for the most classic Argyll diamond-check knitted into lambswool waistcoats and slipovers.

Trousers are never quite so straightforward; success hangs on the size range and shapes. The sort with the most potential are the most old-fashioned; the thick corduroys with button flies, brace loops and a high waist to keep farmers' kidneys warm, in country shades of olive green and donkey brown.

Men's leather jackets are often more of a classic buy than the female kind. The shape to go for is a simple tough leather or suede blouson, like a motorbike jacket. (Avoid any knitted collar, cuffs or hem, which don't last with the leather.) It is well worth looking for a second-hand one, which will have had some character knocked into it for you. Most jackets come in brown or black, but a good source for brighter red, green, white or blue leathers is a motorbike equipment shop. They are certainly not cheap, but definitely count as investment buys.

For alternative evening dress, try the legendary black tuxedo; a classic black jacket, which looks more striking if it is not too oversized, with curved satin lapels, and narrow trousers with satin side stripes. Dinner suits, or tuxedos, are expensive to buy, so you can hire one for special occasions, or look for a second-hand one from dress-hire shops. The sharp lines need feminizing with soft ruffles, a bright cummerbund, a lace or spotted handkerchief and elegant high sandals. If you prefer lower heels, and can find a pair to fit, men's black patent dancing pumps with grosgrain bows make original alternative shoes to wear day or night, especially with white opaque tights. Men's classic felt trilbies or straw panamas are much the easiest and most relaxed kind of hat to wear. Buy them large so they sit well down on the head, or if you have a small head, you could go back to the school uniform department to investigate the straw boaters or winter felt hats.

Tuxedo dressing: immaculate satin striped trousers, dress shirt and white tie by Margaret Howell, worn with a piqué, pearl-studded waistcoat hired from Moss Bros

Try men's pyjamas for alternative summerwear

A man's tartan dressing gown doubles as an original winter coat

The male underwear and nightwear counters have hidden potential. Plain cotton pyjama tops can turn into unexpected shirts, particularly the quality brands that offer contrast piping. Look for delicious combinations of pale pink and white, or white with red, blue, black or yellow. Pyjama tops can be worn buttoned up to the neck, or like an open shirt with the collar turned up or down, and the bottom halves can be transformed into drawstring summer trousers. Traditional wool dressing gowns in unbedroomy, deeply coloured plaids, can adapt into light, winter wrap coats. They look less like a dressing gown, although there is nothing wrong with that, if they are not too long, and the cord is changed for a wider leather belt. It is probably wiser not to wear your pyjama shirt under a dressing gown coat, or you will be irritated by remarks about forgetting to get dressed!

Men's white cotton singlet vests make bargain summer tee shirts, but inspect them first for their depth of armhole as most of them require a low-sided bra underneath. Extra long sizes can be turned into white summer minis. Long and short-sleeved Grandpa vests, with a three-button front, in cream wool or cotton are another alternative top. And if

A lace-edged cotton vest is pretty enough to wear on its own

(Opposite) *in the pink in crisp cotton pyjamas*

Nostalgic cottons (next spread left) *antique lace blouse with Victorian bloomers and lacy cotton knit*

Sea bleached denims (next spread right) *indisputable style if you have the figure to carry it off*

you can find a supply, men's combinations have definite possibilities – as a cuddly boilersuit with sleeves and legs rolled up, or as a warm exercise suit. Leave them cream, or dye them pale pink or blue. Woolly bloomers and long johns also make useful winter jogging pants. Small-sized, cotton boxer shorts can be disguised and worn as brief summer shorts, best in a bright stripe or check that isn't obviously an underwear pattern.

The female underwear department also has concealed promise. If you choose cleverly, certain everyday basics have a double life. In spite of its frumpy image, some thermal underwear is surprisingly pretty. The less thermal it is, the prettier it becomes. The white lacy cotton, fine wool or knitted silk vests are attractive enough to be worn under a loose, low-buttoned shirt, a deep V-neck sweater, or on their own, in place of a tee shirt. If the vest has a ribbon threaded round the neck, you could replace it with a brightly coloured one. An answer to an alternative evening wrap is to try the ladies' bedjacket counter. It may be disastrous, but you might find something rather feminine and appealing like a fluffy angora cardigan slotted with satin ribbon or trimmed with maribou, which, worn out of context, could make a witty and sexy evening jacket.

SPORTING FINDS

Next stop on the alternative shopping expedition is the sports store: shops that specialize in clothes for country pursuits – fishing, riding, shooting, camping and hiking. The coats and jackets are the most versatile buys. Oiled, thornproof, green jackets with check linings are typical of the best country look, but providing they are not mud splattered, they are classic enough to go anywhere. When hacking jackets were an essential in every fashion-conscious wardrobe, the craftiest shoppers bought genuine tweed riding jackets. Others chose boys' tweed sports coats, but the real hacking jackets are a slimmer, more flattering shape, usually in a finer tweed with smart velvet collars. Duffel coats are great value and look good anywhere. The familiar cut of a duffel ranks as a classic coat shape, one that reappears regularly in fashion collections. The best are regulation navy blue with wooden toggles, deep pockets and red tartan lining, worn as a three-quarter coat. The reefer and donkey jacket are more grown-up versions. Both are traditionally navy blue; the reefer is boxy, double breasted with silver buttons; the donkey jacket is more casual, single breasted and tent shaped. Country trouser possibilities are tweedy, corduroy or moleskin (thick brushed cotton) knee breeches or baggier plus fours, to wear with thick, ribbed socks, green gumboots or punched leather lace-ups. Modern jodhpurs are not such a good idea, as they tend to be made of unappealing stretch fabric. But in a surplus store hunt, you may find a rare, old-fashioned, land girl pair in thick cotton or corduroy with buckled waistband and lace-up calves. These should be snapped up immediately.

If you don't feel happy wearing alternative clothes, genuine country accessories should not be overlooked. They are often better made than the fashion equivalent, and certainly better value for money. Sporting bags and baggages come in various sizes and materials, and convert into excellent roomy handbags. Look for canvas fishermen's satchels with strong webbing straps and leather reinforcements, wicker fishing baskets, shooters' cartridge bags and belts, tweed flat caps, equestrian, primrose-yellow string gloves, tough leather hiking shoes or genuine, shiny leather riding boots – horribly expensive, but unbeatable craftsmanship.

From the more active sports wardrobes, cricket clothes can have enormous style. Those attractive cream sweaters, if unobtainable from the school uniform department, can be tracked down, along with cream flannel trousers, striped cricket blazer and peaked cap, in sports outfitters. The best pickings from a golfer's wardrobe are the knitwear. In reality the concept of golfing clothes is based on the thirties-style gentleman golfer, more than today's natty check-trouser pros. The best

Enwrapped in a jumble of treasure – patchwork heirlooms, well-worn cotton smocks and pinafores

Sporting alternatives: hunting, shooting and fishing clothes, worn with a difference

traditional golfer would wear a classic diamond-knit cardigan or slipover, tweed plus fours, Argyll knee socks with fringed corresponding brogues.

The strong link between exercise clothes and fashion has definitely lifted the standards of the design and colour range of keep-fit and sportswear. But there are still separate sources for fashion and exercise clothes, and the sports sources are usually much cheaper. The only drawback is whether you can find tracksuits in plain cotton, towelling or cotton velour, instead of the standard nylon two-piece with a zip jacket and skimpy trousers, both covered in go-faster stripes and emblems. The most wearable shape is a plain, round-necked sweatshirt with generous, cuffed trousers. Both parts look marvellous worn independently when you are not exercising; the trousers with a tee shirt or sweater and high mules, and the top thrown on over anything casual. If you do find simple, cheap, keep-fit clothes, they can be incorporated into your everyday wardrobe. Do remember not to overdo it all, and to mix these clothes with surprising contrasts from other sources. Useful classics are plain white cotton tennis shorts, the Fred Perry polo shirts (worn with a Bryan

Country survival kit: (left) *random layers of thermal vests; oiled wool knitting; long johns; cord, khaki or moleskin breeches; braces; thick ribbed legwarmers; farmer's flat cap; mittens and hiking boots*

On the right track: (right) *flounced leotard, footless tights, satin ballet slippers;* (far right) *the go-anywhere tracksuit, worn together or separately*

An alternative party frock –
a frothy pink tutu

Ferry, lounge-lizard jacket, perhaps), white tennis shoes or track shoes, and practical accessories like divers' watches, headbands and wrist-bands. For dressing up, bright-coloured, scoop-necked leotards look eye-catching worn with full skirts, or if you are brave and have terrific legs, on their own with strappy sandals. Sleeveless leotards can double as athletic swimsuits.

If you can find a shop specializing in dancing clothes, look for ballet practice, knitted leg-warmers, baby wool 'cross-over' cardigans which tie into a bow at the back or front, and original, pastel pink, opaque exercise tights. Satin ballet shoes make beautiful and inexpensive evening slippers in white, shell pink, scarlet or black. In summer try the leather ballet pumps or white lace-up jazz shoes as alternative footwear. If you have secret longings to be a ballerina, you could answer them with a tutu party frock in white, pink or black tulle from the same source. It is pure fancy dress, but can look enchanting if you have the figure and sense of fun to carry it off.

HOME-MADE STYLE

As a more down-to-earth last word, it is unfair to ignore home dressmaking. It is an alternative source of fashion with a guaranteed bonus that everything you make will be an original, and one that is extremely economical. In spite of these incentives, home-made clothes still have a sadly second-rate image – probably because the disastrous efforts stand out as obviously home sewn, and the successes pass effortlessly as shop buys. Providing you aren't overambitious with a complicated pattern, follow every instruction to the letter and never cut any corners, there is no reason for home-made clothes to look amateurish. Sewing does require patience and skill, and you do need to enjoy it. There are pitfalls to beware of; make sure that the material and pattern you choose are right for each other, consider the shape of the design and the way the material falls – thick corduroy won't behave like crepe de Chine. For a professional result it is essential to buy thread, buttons and zips that match the material exactly, and to iron each part as you go along. Once finished, pressing by a dry-cleaner can make all the difference in lifting the home-made stamp. If you are not enthralled by the choice of dressmaking materials, investigate other sources which are often cheaper and more original. Furnishing fabrics are the best alternative, particularly white and cream curtain lining, net, sheeting, mattress ticking, calico, muslin or flower-printed chintzes.

One of the let-downs of home dressmaking can be the limiting choice of paper patterns. It is frustrating to have an idea of what you want to make and not be able to find a corresponding simple pattern. Unless you are a real expert, the experiments where you cut out and sew from a picture or inspiration too often end up in the dustbin. If you want a designer look, it is worth paying a little extra for a fashion name pattern, and making your own Calvin Klein or Perry Ellis, which after all will work out at a fraction of its shop equivalent. Or if you prefer something more original, scour jumble sales, attics and junk shops for job lots of old paper patterns. Sewing straight from an authentic forties, fifties or sixties design is the surest way to genuine alternative fashions.

READING FASHION PICTURES

A fashion magazine can be a valuable source of inspiration for individual style, but how much you get out of it depends on how and why you read it. Some readers treat glossy magazines as an escape from reality into a never-never land where people are beautiful, have perfect figures and live in a tropical paradise or cool white rooms. These readers go into a trance and forget their own lifestyle and budget, and luxuriate in private fantasies of wealth, beauty and stardom. When the pages come to an end they bump back to earth feeling dissatisfied and fed up that magazines never show clothes for ordinary people.

The opposite approach is the magazine addict reader who devours each page like the gospel, accepting everything as the last word on fashion. Unfortunately she often forgets to stop and consider whether the clothes would suit her style, or if she actually likes them. One of my most disillusioning moments while working at *Vogue* was spotting one of these readers who had copied a look slavishly from head to toe. The result was disastrous. She had taken the message literally; lifting it from the page on to herself, detail for detail, colour for colour. Any trace of her own style was swamped by the fashion statement.

The selective reader has a more rational approach. She never loses sight of her image and often buys a magazine because she identifies with the girl on the cover and expects to find corresponding fashion ideas inside. The independent reader has the most relaxed attitude. She is never a slave to magazines and usually flicks backwards through the pages, stopping for a second look at the clothes she likes. Certain ideas sink into her subconscious which may influence her decisions next time she goes shopping.

But whatever the type of reader, most people are too impulsive when they look at a magazine, too quick to dismiss the fashion as ridiculous, unrealistic, exorbitant, or intended for somebody else. These irrational, sweeping decisions make you disgruntled and blind to the point of the

Keep magazine fashion in perspective, treating it as a source of inspiration for your own style

Model faces: the right image helps to project different fashions. In keeping with Fair Isle and tweed, (top left) the natural country face and tousled hair. Polished hair and make-up (top right) match the sophisticated cashmere and pearls. Sultry vamp look (bottom left) for glamorous party dressings. High energy image (bottom right) face glowing with health, boyish no-fuss haircut, athletic figure – just right for sports fashion

fashion in the pictures. The important thing about reading a magazine is balance; between seeing it all as pure wishful thinking, a load of rubbish, or the extreme of following each direction with blind obedience. The point of fashion in a magazine is to tell each reader about as many different options of style and price as possible, and to offer ideas and suggestions. It is not a manifesto that dictates what must be worn each season, but a source of inspiration to help you decide how you would like to look.

It is difficult not to be prejudiced for or against the clothes by the girl inside them. If you identify with the model, or long to look like her, you automatically take more notice of what she is wearing. If you dislike the model, or hate her hairstyle or expression, you are prompted to dismiss the fashion and turn the page. To be entirely neutral the clothes would have to be photographed on coat hangers, but that would remove a lot of their character. The person inside is just as important as the clothes themselves. Even for fashion photographs, it is essential to find a model whose image suits the style of the clothes. If you put glamorous, sophisticated evening dresses on a young, outdoor girl, the moods clash and the picture fails. The image of the model has a powerful effect on the fashion. Unlike the sixties when Twiggy was a household name, models today rarely become individual stars, but their type of hairstyle, make-up and figure can spark off a new look – whether athletic, elegantly polished, nostalgic, countrified or vampish.

What you see in a photograph is a fashion editor and photographer's interpretation of current fashion. The clothes that are featured and the way they are put together are bound to be a subjective choice. There are no definite rules as to what sort of clothes should be shown. One magazine may be showing cowboys, another smart city clothes or ethnic dressing. It does not mean one is behind the other, it is up to the reader to be discerning and choose for herself. Magazines have the power to promote a particular look and equal power to mix clothes and create separate fashions within a fashion. They can invent strange combinations, mixing designer clothes with traditional classics, antiques and sportswear – ideas for the reader to interpret and improvise on herself, without obligation to buy the actual clothes featured.

BEHIND A PHOTOGRAPH

A fashion story starts with a basic idea, usually a theme that focuses on a colour, new proportions, textures, patterns, or clothes for specific occasions. The fashion editor scans the market for appropriate clothes to tell the story. In cheap fashion features, you seldom see an outfit put

together exclusively from one label. Making original looks involves a mix of garments – and adding something unexpected provides extra dash. Luckily fashion editors have the freedom to juggle tops and bottoms to create the right effect. (Fashion advertisements often lack originality and style because they are bound by the confines of selling one brand name.) The outfits that emerge from the selection process are then ready for photography. Once on location, whether in a studio, a house, the countryside, on the street or a tropical beach, the clothes start to live.

But just like real-life dressing, a combination that looked good on a hanger may look uninspiring on the model, and may need some working on. It is time to experiment with different shoes, belts, jewellery, scarves, taking things off and on and off again until it all fits together. Besides the clothes, the hair and make-up are vital ingredients in the final image. Both have to be in keeping with the mood of the clothes and location. Even if they are performed by experts, the most successful fashion pictures give the impression that the face and hair were done by the girl in the picture. A model lolling on a windswept beach with an intricate hair-do and full make-up looks ridiculously artificial.

The most critical ingredient is the photographer. Like top models, the best photographers have a distinctive style which may be more compatible with rugged outdoor fashion than glossy evening dresses, or vice versa. The success of the feature depends strongly on the affinity between the photographer, the model and the fashion itself. The aim is to create a picture that is both artistic and informative. A picture that tells the reader as much as possible about the clothes; the cut, the shape, the texture, the colours, and how to wear them. It can be irritating when art takes over and the clothes are photographed from behind or scrunched up on the floor, or the feet are cropped out of the page, so you have to read about them in the caption instead. But there is a positive angle to these 'mood' pictures. If you like what you see of the clothes, you are forced by necessity to use your imagination and build up the look for yourself.

With most fashion photographs there is a degree of spontaneous invention. Sessions can never be planned like military operations. No one can forecast an exact result until the team joins together, then things that may not occur to the reader can influence the final picture. The size and shape of the model can alter the way the clothes are worn. The pair of shoes that appears on every page could be the only pair that fits her large feet. That ingenious way of wearing a sweater with the V at the back is a successful accident – it looked better back to front so it stayed put. A resourceful hairdresser may devise a new style of fastening a ponytail with a brooch because his last elastic band snapped, or use a tie from a leather sandal to make a headband because it is longer than his ribbon.

Fashion editors can create their own impromptu combinations; mixing designer's clothes with antique lace and lengths of inexpensive materials – ideas to interpret and improvise on

When you realize it is not a cut-and-dried procedure, but one where a strong element of trial and error counts, it makes sense to treat fashion photographs more as a springboard for information and ideas. Too often when a particular garment is featured, the buying public have a distinct imagination failure and rush off to find a duplicate, preferably in the same colour. Not surprisingly shops cash in on publicity and encourage you to buy the duplicate jacket or skirt just because it has appeared in a magazine. That does not make it better than everything else in the shop; there may be similar shapes and colours that will suit you more. (When the garment was photographed, it may only have been available in one sample colour, and not necessarily the prettiest.) It is worth remembering that in black and white photography, the clothes featured are often very pale or white, or very dark colours, because they photograph more sharply than medium colours like mid-blue, red and green.

THE SEASONAL FACTOR

The annoying part of buying high-fashion clothes from magazine features is that by the time they arrive in the shops, which usually coincides with the magazine publication, they are, as far as the fashion experts are concerned, on the wane. The trade latches on to spring and summer fashion in October, and autumn and winter fashion in March, and there is nothing to stop you doing the same. Twice a year the collections in London, Paris, Milan and New York are given wide press coverage. As magazines work three or four months in advance, newspapers supply the instant fashion reports. The trouble is that it is hard to feel enthusiasm and interest for clothes relevant to a season we have just been through. But it is well worth studying the reports and digesting the new details, themes and colours which, with skill, can be used ahead of time. What you buy for summer can be influenced by your knowledge of the winter collections. It is a really useful idea to cut out and keep pictures of the styles you like, and use them as a guideline. If you are not a regular magazine buyer, the most informative issues to read are those with a summary of the coming season's fashion – issues which usually coincide with new stock in the shops. If you can find them, foreign fashion magazines, especially the French, Italian and American ones are worth looking at. The fashion stories offer a different viewpoint, and because the price and stockists are irrelevant, you take more notice of the clothes, colours, and the way everything goes together.

The most habitual complaints from magazine readers are that most of the clothes featured are too expensive. Magazines do not set out to torture their readers with unrealistic prices. The fact that the most striking fashion features consist of expensive clothes is often hard to avoid. Very often they are the only ones of their kind yet in existence, and have to be used to tell the story. Probably by the time the magazine appears on the bookstalls there are similar versions at lower prices. Magazines also have a duty to provide fashion information. Given the choice between a beautifully made pair of dark navy trousers in fine wool gaberdine and a badly cut, royal navy pair in polyester gaberdine, they will select the expensive version as an example of the best of a kind. Careful photography with cheap clothes can be disillusioning; they can look terrific in the picture, but tatty in a shop. Not necessarily because they have been photographed through a misty lens, but because they have been worn imaginatively and mixed with original, more expensive accessories. The usual fault with cheap fashion is the skimpiness of cut, something which can be disguised by putting the model in a size twelve or fourteen instead of a ten. A more generous shape with coats, jackets, shirts and trousers immediately adds more style and improves the look of the clothes.

Reading a magazine is like visiting more than one shop. There are

Experiment in shops by trying on a larger size than usual. With certain styles a more generous, loose-fitting shape can prevent cheap clothes looking mean and skimpy

Designer influence: Chloé's strong silhouette inspires high-street copies

The genuine Chloé: plunging yellow cardigan, piqué strapless top, black grosgrain skirt, patent belt and lacquered straw saucer hat

More dash than cash à la Chloé: echoing the vital plunge neckline, defined shiny waist and narrow skirt

usually two or three fashion options to consider with different styles and price tags. But being confined to the cheap pages should not stop you benefiting from the expensive pages. If you study them, you start to recognize the handwriting of top designers and notice how their influence filters through to the cheaper market. You are ready to spot a knock-off Perry Ellis, Chloé, Basile; and a well-made knock-off is the next best thing to the real thing.

KEY DETAILS

Now there are so few overnight sensations, it is often the details of how the clothes are put together that make fashion news. These details, not always immediately obvious, can update what appears at first to be yet another feature about coats or jackets. After the initial browse through a magazine, you need to look back with a more fashion-conscious eye for the key details. Start with the overall shape. Is the silhouette narrow, layered, voluminous or fitted? Then check proportions; scrutinize the lengths and shapes of skirts, trousers, coats, jackets, knitwear and how they measure against each other. Are the skirts longer with loose blazers, shorter with cropped jackets? Do the trousers skim the ankle bone, or fall in folds over the shoes, and are the heels high or low? Where is the strongest focus? Is the eye drawn to square, curved, dropped or exaggerated shoulders? Is the waist accentuated, or is the hip line more noticeable? Do the knees feature at all? How are the clothes structured? Is the look tailored, ruffled, or soft and fluid? Notice how the clothes fit the body; is everything neat and fitted or loosely wrapped?

Then check the finer points. Notice every accessory, storing up ideas you like as you go along, watching the context of the clothes and the way each accessory is used, not just what they look like as individual objects. Is jewellery an important part of the style, or is it unnecessary? Is there emphasis on one thing – a special brooch, long pearls, heavy bangles, spectacular earrings, a blanket shawl, a diver's watch, a hair accessory? Is one recurrent belt the mainstay of a particular look – a wrapped sash, a neat, narrow leather belt that discreetly defines the waist, or a bright cummerbund that is a focal point?

While you check the accessories in each picture, think about what has been left out. An essential side of accessorizing is also what you leave off the clothes. The statement often has more impact by reducing accessories to the minimum. When you see a photograph without any accessories, it is not that the fashion editor forgot to take them with her, but because the clothes do not need any embellishments or distractions.

Shoes, socks, tights or stockings are permanent accessories that

Key proportions: (left) *long and narrow at Perry Ellis, or short and ruffled at Kenzo*

Footwear update: (right) *surprise flat black pumps with pale stockings under Ralph Lauren's swirling skirt. Unexpected, but new looking, dark tights and walking shoes with Jean Muir's dress and chamois coat*

always indicate a fashion message. New shapes, colour, density and texture immediately update one look into another. Heel heights alter the whole proportions. There are still fixed associations with shoe types: low heels with coloured textured tights spell relaxed, informal dressing, and elegant high heels with sheer, neutral tights spell smarter, grown-up dressing. But footwear can provide the unexpected twist that updates a classic style into something new. Suddenly putting flat country shoes and thick tights where you expect to find high shoes and fifteen-denier stockings can be the difference between last year's style and this year's.

When you find a look that you like, besides studying the actual clothes, notice how they are worn. It can be the smallest details that make them stand out. The points to check may sound insignificant, but they are what counts. Little details like whether the sleeves of a shirt, tee shirt or jacket are rolled back; whether a collar is turned up or down; whether a jacket is belted or left unbuttoned; which tops are tucked into skirts or trousers, which are left loose, which ones belted. Whenever a belt features, how is it worn? Is a coat or raincoat belted with a self belt or a different one? How is the scarf tied; like a muffler, a kerchief, a headband? Must it be a square or oblong to work that way?

It is important to distinguish between these subtle finishing touches and shortlived fashion gimmicks; the looks that stand out at the time

Focal points: belt emphasis at
Calvin Klein; (left) hips wrapped
wide and buckled to one side, or
waists bound with scarves, then
belted

More waist details at Ralph
Lauren: (below) swathes of
sacking topped with tan leather

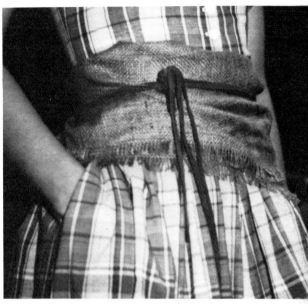

Fashion extremes – a lethal exaggeration of styling: mini coats in 1969 with oversized collars, lapels, pockets and belts

Timeless classics: with contemporary hair and make-up, this 1965 Fair Isle sweater would look quite in keeping today

because they are extremes, but date overnight when the next craze arrives, and feel like history five years later. Anyone can learn to spot a fleeting, but newsworthy look. The key point is an exaggeration of styling – clothes with completely opposite qualities to a classic.

The shoe cycle is an example. Fashions for platform soles, wedges and stilettos occur sporadically and each time round are worn for their novelty value, but when the look reverts to a naturally elegant, thin-soled, fine-heeled shoe, the other styles seem like monstrous, clumpy gimmicks.

See-sawing hemlines are another obvious fashion extreme. Looking back at the late sixties and seventies it is almost possible to tell the year by the length of the skirts. Now the shapes and proportions are more telling than hemlines. The critical details to watch – not difficult, as exaggerations tend to hit you in the eye – are overemphasized lapels, oversized collars and cuffs, unnatural shoulder shapes, trouser widths,

Gimmick looks – fun while they last. In 1974 (right) it was hectic accessories and clumpy platform soles

High fashion classics do move with the times: (above) the 1980 mini; (far right) the 1965 mini

Remember that a collection is shown as a total fashion look: in Montana's case complete with theatrical accessories and traffic-stopping hair and make-up

turn-ups, wide waistbands, contrived details like top stitching and excessive trimming. They are all danger spots prone to overdesigning.

The pattern is apparent when you look at back copies of fashion magazines and pick out the most dating aspects of the clothes. With true classics, the only part that dates is the way the fashion is put together, with accessories, hair and make-up typical of the year. Taken out of context and updated, the same clothes – a trench coat, a sweater and shirt, a blazer – can all look quite in keeping today. But the high-fashion extremes just make us laugh and feel amazed that anyone could actually have walked around looking so extraordinary. Gimmicks, which at the time were the key fashion details, show up as ugly, unnatural sensations. There are high-fashion classics which reappear in a style to suit the new climate. The mini of the sixties was a straight shift, pinafore, or little suit which went with shiny boots, and has re-emerged for the eighties as an overgrown sweater, an elongated ruffled shirt or flounced skirt to go with flat suede boots or ballet pumps.

One thing to remember is that from a magazine viewpoint an extreme fashion with a definite message is a news story which, as an information service, it is their duty to pass on. A photograph illustrating the total look from one designer is a faithful reproduction of how he or she sent the models down the catwalk. A collection is shown as a fashion package, complete with theatrical accessories where needed and larger-than-life hair and make-up. It is often an extreme statement which the designer knows will be diluted and rearranged with other fashion, but one that puts the point of the new collection across.

INSIDE STYLE

No clothes, however beautiful, can detract from a neglected physical appearance. An unhealthy body and unkempt skin and hair ruin everything. To look great you have to feel great, and that means looking after yourself, inside and out. You need the natural self-confidence that comes from a state of inner well-being. It all demands the right attitude to yourself, one that banishes any idea that a pre-occupation with health and appearance is self-indulgent. Looking after yourself is the best investment possible, one that requires more time and effort than money. It means incorporating a health and beauty routine into your lifestyle, so that it becomes second nature, but never an obsession. You may have to work out a new balance, like getting up ten minutes earlier to fit in a morning skin-care routine, or to wash your hair or repaint your nails. You need the self-discipline to find time for a proper night's sleep and a healthy breakfast, to keep a dental appointment, to find a bra that fits perfectly, all of which becomes easier if you see them as pleasures rather than chores, and accept that looking good involves consistent effort. Even born beauties have to work at staying beautiful. It is not something to take for granted – 'Il faut souffrir pour être belle,' as French mothers preach to their daughters.

To keep things in perspective, it is important to understand the basic principles of good health: how the body is affected by day to day living; what is good for the system and what is harmful; that it is possible to maintain a healthy state without cranky dieting and anti-social habits. Moderation is sensible – and necessary if you are to keep the constant wave of health hazard revelations in proportion. According to news-papers, magazines and television documentaries, there are dangers lurking in the most innocent products – tea, coffee, eggs, butter, suntan lotion, hairspray – but virtually everything in unbalanced quantities is unhealthy, even health foods. If we reacted to every scare, life would be no fun at all.

To look great you have to feel great, and that means looking after yourself inside and out

How much you spend on beauty products is a matter of choice. With clothes you know immediately what you are paying for. You choose the colour and the shape, you can tell what a particular garment does for you. When you choose beauty products, whether skin care, hair care, cosmetics, or sun products, the price and the advertising are the only guidelines. It is tempting to be seduced by the glamorous image that comes with high-priced products. When you treat yourself to expensive brands, you feel rather special. The effect can be more psychological than directly beneficial to your skin or hair. High-priced products are not automatically superior to cheaper ones; you may be paying extra for advertising, smart packaging and a prestige name. How much more efficient expensive brands are is a controversial point. Basically the various types of product perform the same function; some higher priced ones *may* be more sophisticated and scientifically advanced, and therefore some people would say superior. But if you like the performance and texture of an inexpensive brand, so much the better. The key point is to find a range that works for you and then stay with it. In any event go for the pure, non-scented types – baby products are unbeatable for economy and purity. Whatever your budget, it is essential to portion it carefully across all your demands. But if you have one problem area, be it skin or hair, it obviously qualifies for special attention, especially if the problem affects your self-confidence.

SKIN

Skin is the first area that reacts against poor treatment. Its condition is a giveaway to your state of well-being. Facial skin is the most vulnerable, and its sensitivity varies with everyone, but most faces are affected by certain external and internal conditions – harsh temperatures, cold or hot sun, strong winds, drying atmosphere from central heating, air conditioning, long contact with water or strong detergents. From inside, it is affected by diet, smoking, alcohol, stress, fatigue, illness, hormone balance and erratic sleep patterns.

Whatever your skin type, a consistent **skin care programme** is crucial. It should be as automatic as brushing teeth, twice a day. Vital stages are cleansing, toning, and moisturizing. All faces, however dry they seem, have a T-zone of oilier skin across the forehead and down the nose and chin. This area is the most prone to spots and disorders because it has the highest density of sebaceous glands. Unless skin in the zone is kept scrupulously clean, oily secretions from the glands can block the pores and encourage spots and blackheads. Trouble can be aggravated, and even caused, by absentminded habits of holding and touching the chin.

Every inch of skin on the face and body deserves consistent care

Cleansing can be done in two stages; the first with a cream or lotion that dissolves make-up, the second with mild acid-balanced soap which is the most efficient and underrated method of removing stubborn grime and the left-over greasiness of the cleanser. The soap must be specifically for the face as ordinary soap has a high alkaline content which strips the natural protective moisture from the skin.

Toning stimulates the circulation, closes the pores and helps to prevent a build-up of dead flaky skin. Dry or sensitive skins should avoid astringent toners with an alcohol content, or any product that stings. All toners are too strong for the eye area.

Moisturizing is the essential protective stage. It helps prevent water loss from the skin by sealing in the natural moisture and keeping the surface smooth. Rough, dry skin is a sign of dehydration. Moisturizer is an essential guard against the external enemies and should be applied before the skin is subjected to extreme environments, or sudden changes from one temperature to another. It is wise to carry a tube around with you and use it whenever your skin feels dry or tight, but always in small quantities. Overloading your face with moisturizer leaves it feeling puffy and can block the pores, especially last thing at night. The eye area is particularly vulnerable and needs delicate cleansing with a specific eye make-up remover, and moisturizing with a tiny amount of eye cream. Lips need permanent protection against chapping with a lipsalve, which in summer should contain a sunscreen. The neck is too often neglected but qualifies for the same regular treatment as your face.

Long baths are wonderfully relaxing, but soaking in water draws natural moisture from the skin – the hotter the water, the harsher the action. **Bath oil** and body lotion help to counteract the drying process. Showers are kinder to the skin than long baths. There is no time for any skin damage, and the force of the water braces the circulation. Whenever you wash the body, use products that match the skin's chemistry. Skin is covered with a protective layer called an acid mantle; a delicate barrier which has to be kept intact by maintaining its correct pH balance. (The pH scale runs from 0, acid, to 14, alkaline.) Most mantles contain an equal, or slightly acid biased, balance producing a pH between 4 and 5 – which is broken down by high pH alkaline detergents – the kinds of soap and bubble baths that lather profusely and leave the skin feeling taut and itchy. Once destroyed, the mantle takes twelve hours to replace itself but during that vulnerable time skin needs extra protective moisturizing and care. Skin renewal is a constant process, too often indicated by dry, scaly patches on the body – areas of dead skin ready to be sloughed away with a loofah, scrubbing brush or exfoliating soap.

The cumulative dangers of **sunbathing** have taken some of the cachet away from a suntan. Now instead of feeling unattractive and lily-white,

Wake up with a shower: bracing and far kinder to the skin than a long hot bath

you can justify a pale skin with the proven argument that you intend to stay looking young with soft, wrinkle-free skin. But providing you treat your skin like a baby's when you do go in the sun, the psychological boost of being brown is undeniable. A suntan, particularly out of season, does make you glow with a feeling of health and self-confidence. It is the best example of how magical proper self-indulgence can be. A suntan does not have to be a dark chocolate brown, it is safer and just as stunning to toast yourself to a pale honey colour.

Whatever shade your tan, the sun is the skin's worst enemy, so to minimize danger it is essential to understand the mechanics of a suntan. Build up a tan gradually with the constant protection of a sunscreen which filters out harmful ultraviolet rays and lets through the ultraviolet tanning rays in small doses. Turning brown is the body's protective reaction to the sun. The brown is actually a pigment in the skin called melanin which is activated by ultraviolet light. The amount of brown pigment varies with each skin type and determines your sensitivity to the sun. Fair skins produce less melanin than dark ones, so they are more susceptible to sunburn and need a correspondingly high degree of protection. If you have very fair or sensitive skin which cannot tolerate sun at all, resign yourself to staying pale, feminine and in no danger of skin damage. Capitalize on a delicate complexion, which was after all the yardstick of beauty for centuries, and shade yourself behind a wide-brimmed straw panama and cream tulle veiling. Sunburn is a sign of skin damage. Sore red skin is not the natural beginning of a tan, it may turn brown, but will peel fast, especially after a bath or swim. Even when you are not consciously sunbathing, the strength of the sun is the same and attacks any exposed areas of skin. If you are caught unaware, the only answer is to go inside or cover yourself in more clothes. In hot climates the shade can be almost as treacherous as direct sunlight. Constant protection is *essential*, it is never worth taking a risk, even for five minutes.

BODY MAINTENANCE

Understand the science of sunbathing and build up your tan gradually with constant protection from a sunscreen

Like being brown, being fit is pure pleasure. **Fitness** that comes from regular exercise is exhilarating. You feel in control of your body, become more aware of movements, gestures, posture. Exercise is a great stimulation for both body and mind. Inactivity saps energy and makes you feel heavy and lethargic. Fitness breeds energy, making you more alive, more spontaneous, less inclined to laze about and yawn all the time. It is so satisfying to find enough energy to run effortlessly for a bus without gasping for breath, purple in the face. To stay fit, exercise has to

Exercise is a marvellous tonic for the mind and body. Choose a sport you enjoy and can afford to practise, and one that fits into your lifestyle

be a regular, preferably daily, part of your life, but not an obsession. Concentrate on a sport that you enjoy and one that is easily accessible and cheap to practise. If you lead a town life, best options are indoor sports like squash, badminton, swimming, keep-fit, gymnastics, dance classes or yoga. With outdoor sports, fresh air helps to boost the sense of well-being; jogging, cycling, swimming, tennis, riding, sailing are all great fitness prompters. At the very least it should be possible to incorporate extra exercise into a normal daily routine, but discipline yourself. Get into the habit of walking everywhere, ignore lifts and use the stairs instead, start to run somewhere every day, even if there is no hurry, or try skipping, or running on the spot for five minutes daily.

Exercise revs the circulation, the essential body process that makes skin glow with health and speeds up the metabolic rate, the process that burns calories. When you stop exercising your metabolism is still racing and goes on demolishing body fat at a faster than normal rate for up to six hours. It is a myth that exercise alone makes you lose weight. It tones muscle, changes flab into firm body and gives you an incentive to eat healthier food. It is a waste of effort and time to fill a well-conditioned body with stodgy food. A diet combined with an exercise programme is the most logical way to slim – the two processes complement each other. In some people a lack of exercise is more cause for fatness than overeating.

WHAT MAKES A GREAT BODY

It is rare to meet anyone who is content with their size, shape and weight. Statistics tell us that one in three women is on a **diet**. Many base their reasons for dieting on irrational grounds. The most common cause of misery is when you compare yourself with someone the same height, who weighs a stone less than you and takes a smaller size. What gets overlooked is the fundamental build of a body; providing you are in proportion to your frame, measuring or weighing more than the next person is not a sign of being overweight. There is no such thing as the ideal stereotype female. A perfect body may be athletic, petite, curvy, or sticklike. You have to be realistic and accept, to a certain extent, the shape that nature intended for you. It is more attractive to feel positive about the way you are, than struggle on in permanent battle trying to be somebody different. The only judge of your figure is you; if you hate your body and have the willpower to improve it, without damaging your health or personality and without losing friends, then go ahead.

The quickest way to lose weight is to go on a crash diet, but it is a short-term solution. The pounds you lose consist of water and body fluids

Exercise combined with a healthy, balanced diet generates irrepressible energy

which return when you eat normally again. Most 'miracle' diets are doomed; the mentality of consciously cutting out bad foods for a limited time until the goal weight is achieved is disastrous. The idea that when you are on a diet you eat healthy food, and when you are off a diet you can eat junk food, is schizophrenic. While you diet you feel deprived and plan enormous binges of chocolate cake and lasagne. It turns into an unnecessary battle. Losing weight painlessly needs a different approach. The sensible alternative is to follow a well-balanced diet all the time. The constant preoccupation with health and diet has turned nutrition into a rather fashionable science – once you start being aware of what you eat, it is dangerously easy to become fanatical about your diet. A balanced diet should not be cranky or extreme. There is room for a little of everything. Food is something to enjoy, and eating sensibly does not automatically rule out all treats. When you understand the nutritional and calorific value of different foods it is simple enough to eat healthily and lose weight if necessary by consuming fewer calories. Diets may vary, but the basic principle of losing weight never does. If you take in more than you burn off as energy, you will put on weight.

A **healthy diet** should provide essential vitamins and minerals and include a balance of protein (meat, fish, eggs, cheese), fresh fruit and vegetables, cereals (wholemeal bread, muesli, brown rice, bran), and a small amount of fats (butter, vegetable oil, low-fat cheese). Fresh fruit and vegetables are a great low-calorie source of energy. The healthiest way to eat them is raw, as cooking removes some valuable vitamins and minerals. Raw fruit and vegetables are perfect for dieters because their high water content (much of which is lost in the cooking) makes them very filling.

Healthy eating means training yourself into good habits. It makes sense to eat a proper breakfast as you are bound to burn up the calories during the day. Three equal meals is a better balance than one great binge, but ideally your lightest meal should be at night. The metabolic rate slows down while you sleep, and any excess food, particularly carbohydrates like bread and pudding, is quickly stored as fat.

One habit to get into is drinking as much water as possible, at least a pint a day. It is the healthiest drink there is, calorie free and essential for energy and clear skin. Alcohol in moderation is not unhealthy, but it is astonishingly high in calories. White sugar contains no goodness at all and should be cut out of a diet. Honey is a better substitute. Even chocolate has some useful proteins and can be eaten occasionally without too much guilt.

Nutritional value is affected by the cooking methods. Grilling, boiling or steaming is healthier than frying in oil or butter. Too much fried food is bad for the skin, particularly if it is naturally oily. The connection

Food is something to enjoy: sensible eating does not mean depriving yourself of all treats

between skin condition and diet affects some people much more than others. There is no doubt that skin thrives on a steady intake of vitamins and minerals from fresh, natural foods and can be disturbed by stimulants like strong coffee, hot spicy foods, too much alcohol, sugar or nicotine. Food allergies are unpredictable and idiosyncratic, but often a skin disorder can be traced to a deficiency or excess in the diet. Because everyone is different, it is impossible to make rules about these allergies – specialists are still arguing over the link between chocolate and pimples.

HAIR

Hair needs as much consistent attention as skin. Like skin, the state of your hair is a sign of your well-being. Hair responds to the right diet, regular sleep, well-charged circulation and scrupulous cleansing and care. Hair needs to be treated with the same respect as your face, never antagonized with fierce equipment and whatever product comes to hand. It needs protection from its worst enemies: from the sun with a hat, scarf or special sun-filtering conditioner; from salt water and chlorine by rinsing after swimming in fresh water; from hot rollers, heated tongs and hot blasts of air from hairdryers. Hair is at its most fragile when wet, and should never be brushed, but untangled with a wide-toothed comb. Long hair is more vulnerable than short hair simply because it is in the way, and slept upon, fiddled with, pulled at much more than short hair can be.

Your hair type determines how often you need to shampoo. Daily washing is quite safe providing the shampoo is mild. One soaping with a small quantity of shampoo is enough. Conditioner helps to add shine by smoothing the scales on the hair shaft, making hair smoother and better behaved. Dry, brittle, split or damaged ends benefit from a deeper treatment which penetrates the hair shaft and helps restore its condition. It is essential to rinse off the conditioner thoroughly which, in soft water, can be a long process, otherwise hair goes limp and greasy almost immediately.

Hair can only look good if it is well kept. The emphasis has now moved away from sculptured 'hair-dos' to a natural look which relies on hair health. It is *the* foundation, however you wear your hair. The mood of fashion and hair are inseparable, hair has to be part of a total look. The most crucial point is for hair to suit your personality, never to take over as a fashion statement. It must fit in with you, but not as a permanent fixture. You can rethink your hair as often as you change your clothes or make-up; often a switch of hairstyle is all that's needed to change the pace of your look. Hair should never be a burden. The attitude must be easy care, style with minimum maintenance, a shape that doesn't need

Hair deserves the same careful treatment and protection as your skin

hours of upkeep with damaging rollers or fixing with hairspray. You need a style that can be out in the wind and the rain; that you can wash on the spur of the moment and shake dry; a style that boosts your confidence about your whole appearance.

The vital guideline is to know how your hair performs; how much the texture and condition dictate the final appearance. If your hair is naturally straight, forget about curling it, if it is frizzy, then let it frizz. Choose a style compatible with your hair type as well as your character. Beware of being blinded by a fashion, or inspired by a cut that looks marvellous on someone else. If long, glossy hair is your great pride, don't let yourself be swept along on a wave of boyish cuts; you may regret it – especially as average hair grows only six inches a year. There *may* come a time when after years of experimenting with different shapes and lengths, you find the look that is absolutely perfect for you – one that makes you feel terrific, sexy and self-confident enough to like your face without any help from make-up. When and if this does happen to you, it makes sense to hold on to the style and experiment no further.

Thick straight hair is the most versatile, as it can look good worn any length or style. Long, thick, curly hair looks wonderful worn full like a Pre-Raphaelite, or piled loosely into a tousled knot on top. Very bushy hair is more controllable cut shorter and softly layered. Medium-textured hair is also full of possibilities: if straight, a layered cut adds fullness; if curly, layering helps to bring out the curl, or keeping it one length plays it down. Fine hair tends to be limp and flyaway; straight fine hair looks prettiest in a chin-length blunt cut, or in a wispy short crop. Fine curly hair looks fuller if it is cut in slightly ragged layers.

Hair should not be treated as a means to alter the shape of a face. The suggested corrective style may conflict with the natural tendency of the hair texture, your personality or facial features and you end up with an unsatisfactory compromise. Whatever the shape of the face, it is an important characteristic, and not something to camouflage. But there are some routine guidelines to balance a hairstyle with different face shapes and features – most of which are based on logic. It makes sense not to swamp a small face and delicate features with an overpowering mass of hair; a neater shape swept away from the face works well. Square and round faces need balancing with some extra height on top, and softening with wispy, all-over volume. A wide jaw can be minimized by a style that falls in layers round the face and a shaggy fringe to draw the eyes upwards. A thin face can be softened with extra width at the sides.

Promoting your best features also makes sense; a side parting emphasizes the eyes, and a centre parting emphasizes the nose and mouth. Short hair is easier to look after than long; it is quicker to wash and dry, but it does need to be kept in good shape with a trim every four to

Know how your hair performs: understand how its natural texture and condition affect the final style

Experiment with long hair by sweeping it up into a loose top knot

Easy-care shock of hair: a boyish shape that needs regular trimming

six weeks. The cut itself is critical. A precise, clipped cut looks severe and too neat. The best haircut doesn't look too obvious, it is left soft and wispy enough to avoid a fresh-from-the-barber look. Layered hair demands more upkeep than one-length shapes. Even if you decide to grow out a layered cut, the only way to carry it off is with regular trims to keep the lengths close together. The longest straggly bits are best cut off, as they look out of proportion and messy otherwise. When hair is left to look natural, there has to be a definite difference between a wayward, tousled head and a matted bird's nest.

Drying hair in different ways can alter the appearance as well. Straightforward blow drying and brushing with a good bristle brush (once the hair is nearly dry) gives a smooth, glossy finish. For a more mane-like effect with a hairdryer, you should bend at the waist and blow the roots from underneath which fluffs up the hair and adds extra volume. Another hairdresser's tip for fullness is to spray the roots with liquid setting lotion which adds extra body and makes the hair stand away from the head. Finger drying, a technique your hairdresser should teach you, is the most natural and gentle way to dry. Start with a towel to squeeze out surface moisture, then let your fingers take over.

Although the actual process of hair colour is highly scientific (unless you choose henna) the result, if done by an expert, can be beautifully natural. The best kind of hair colouring is one which is not too striking, one which uses subtle streaks or lowlights (less obvious than highlights) that enhance your original colour. It is wise to base any change on a colour close to your natural hair colour. A dramatic change can look artificial and you suffer from noticeable regrowth. Tinted hair needs extra special care and conditioning, but professionally applied colour does not do any damage, it can even thicken the texture of fine hair, making it more manageable. When you have colour on your hair, it is sensitive to certain chemicals and can react curiously against further tinting, perming, or even strong sunlight.

The condition of your hair is controlled by you, but its shape is left in the hands of the hairdresser. A success with your hair is much more likely if you go regularly to the same person. He or she gets to know you and your hair and understand what you like. A small friendly salon is usually less intimidating than a large, impersonal place (even if it does have a grand name) where you may be treated like a number to be processed on your first few visits.

The greatest cause of post-haircut misery is a lack of communication. Hairdressers are not mindreaders. It is essential to explain exactly what you want and how much you want cut off, before it is too late. Whenever possible, discuss the style with the hairdresser before you are shampooed, so he sees how your hair looks and falls when dry. If you are

An elongated 'short cut', softly layered into a most feminine crop

thinking of a new haircut it is a good idea to take a picture with you, as long as you don't expect to emerge looking identical. Your hair type may not suit the shape, but it is a good starting point to work from, especially if you find explaining difficult. When you try a new salon it is worth finding out the price before you make an appointment. Watch out for extras like conditioning treatments and special rinses, which can be done just as effectively at home for a fraction of the salon price using similar products from a chemist, not the expensive salon brands. Some salons run special nights when their juniors practise on the clients. If you need a simple trim it is a good way to have a cheap haircut. The juniors are usually closely supervised by the experts, who take over in an

emergency. Be wary about letting yourself be a guinea pig for any creative colouring or styling. Mistakes *can* happen.

Once you have the basis of a good cut and condition, you can treat your hair, long or short, like a versatile accessory. Experiment; change the parting to create a different effect, or try to lose it completely. Experiment with plaits; try one thick one taken from the crown of your head, two schoolgirl braids tied with bright ribbon, or a crowd of tiny plaits to release at night into a crinkly mass. Try ponytails: fifties style, high on the head, or Chanel style, smoothed into the nape of the neck with a velvet bow. See how you look with your hair up, but whatever you do should be completely natural and not glued with hairspray or thick with pins. Hair has to move with you; abandon any style that looks good only if you keep still. Short hair has just as much scope. You need a variety of accessories to change its appearance: ribbons, combs, feathers, slides, bootlaces. Try an Alice-band with a bow on top, a mini ponytail, or fold a cotton scarf into a bandana and wear as a headband, Mohican style. Be inventive with the materials: plait bright satin ribbons together to make a hair band, make a party bow from spangly tulle, wind coloured pipe cleaners, nail-varnished chop sticks or knitting needles into your hair. Move from the haberdashery to the Christmas decoration department and investigate festive silver and gold parcel rosettes, tiny baubles, anything that sparkles, and turn them into hair ornaments. For a sleeker look, try slicking back short hair with gentlemen's hair oil or brilliantine.

COSMETICS

The last stage of self-care concerns **cosmetics**. They cannot disguise unloved skin. Whether you wear full make-up or the faintest trace, a healthy glowing skin is the starting point. The rest is individual choice, one that can be extremely bewildering when you are confronted with an enormous range of temptingly named and packaged cosmetics. Such a selection of products, colours and textures makes it easy to make mistakes and waste money. Knowing how to get the most from make-up is an immeasurable asset. The instant proof is to watch top models. When they arrive on location they are often indistinguishable from anyone else. Fashion editors have been known to mistake the model for a tea girl. But once made up, they look perfect, just like a model in fact. Not because they are caked in theatrical make-up, but because they have acquired the professional expertise to transform an ordinary face into a beautiful one. It is a skill within the reach of everybody who cares enough to make an effort. Few people get the full potential from the

Minimum upkeep – choose a style that doesn't rule your life. You need hair that goes out in the wind and rain without being a worry; that you can wash and shake dry on impulse

cosmetics they use and miss out on the incredible bonus that cleverly applied make-up can give. The essential skill is learning basic techniques; understanding the difference that the actual method makes to the result. Being clever with fancy products is like trying to run before you can walk. What counts most is knowing how to make the best of your face, naturally. Make-up is not a camouflage to be treated like a mask, but an accessory to experiment with and change with different clothes, seasons and environments.

There are times when make-up is unnecessary. It is important not to depend so heavily on it that you feel insecure without any. Make-up should never take over from your natural expression. The point is to make your *face* more striking, not the make-up. Once you have learnt the basics, an open-minded attitude is a must. See the make-up you wear as a way of pulling your whole look together, and adding new dimension to your clothes. Avoid the habit of treating it as a routine. Vary the amount you use, go barefaced when you don't feel like make-up, and don't apologize for your naked face . . .

Buying cosmetics is an indulgence. Few people actually run out of anything, but treat themselves to a new product for the fun of it, and because it is a cheaper self-indulgence than buying clothes. But however much you buy, most good make-ups rely on a few basic products. Like skin care, the final price can be more a reflection of the pretty packaging and prestige name than the actual ingredients of the cosmetic. The performance of different brands varies widely, and if you shop around it is possible to find similar colours and textures in less impressive pots and boxes which do the same job as the expensive versions. It is worth taking time to try the testers. If possible, go to a large department store or chemist that stocks a cross section of brands, so you can compare prices and colours. Salesgirls affiliated to a particular brand name are there to sell you their products, so don't be too easily swayed. Make your own decisions. If you are contemplating an expensive product, it is worth buying a trial size to start with. Some department stores run promotions when they offer a free make-up to anyone brave enough to face the public stare. It can be a humiliating experience, but worth undergoing, because, although the make-up artist usually puts far too much on, you can learn some basic make-up skills. When you get home, try removing one side of the make-up and applying your own products. If you have a free lesson, don't feel obliged to restock with brand-new products. Go through your collection first, as you may already own a similar cosmetic that you can adapt and use instead.

The best investment is the right equipment. The difference between a professional and amateur make-up is how the products are used and what they are applied with. A model's make-up bag is incomplete

Take care not to overplay your eyes, as a heavy make-up can kill their natural expression. Keep to a palette of subtle, muted colours – well smudged and blended, with no hard lines anywhere

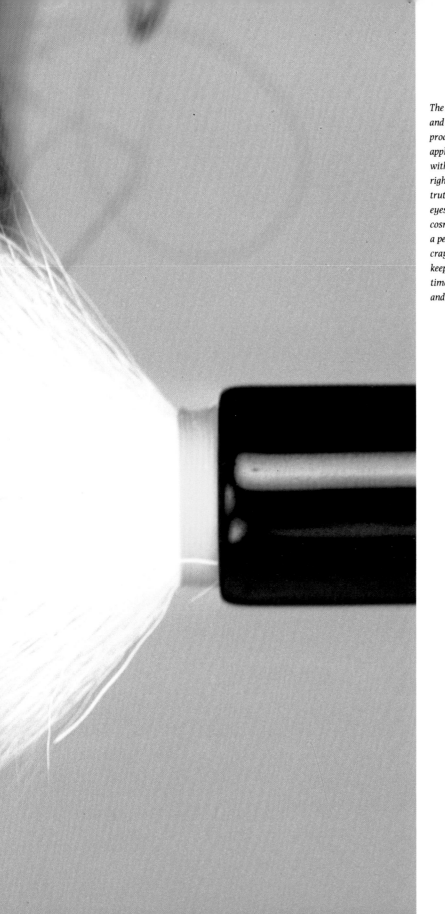

The difference between a professional
and amateur make-up is how the
products are used, and what they are
applied with. Give yourself a headstart
with the right equipment and the
right approach. You need a well lit,
truthful mirror, a set of brushes for
eyes, lips, blusher and powder;
cosmetic sponges; cotton buds; tissues;
a pencil sharpener for your cosmetic
crayons; a towelling band or scarf to
keep hair off your face; and plenty of
time to complete each stage slowly
and carefully

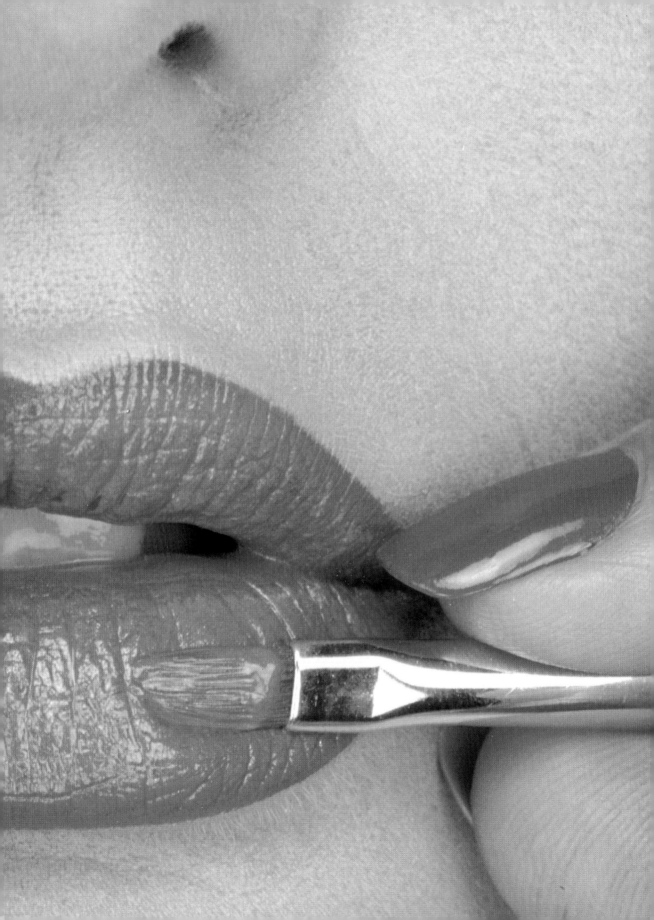

without a set of brushes, one for each stage. Sable brushes are expensive, but definitely worth the outlay. If you look after them carefully, they will not wear out, but for an alternative source, investigate paint brushes in an art supply shop. Give yourself a head start by not scrimping on the basic necessities. Besides brushes, you need small, cosmetic sponges, good tweezers, cotton buds, cotton wool and a truthful mirror. A magnifying mirror is a wise investment and invaluable for plucking eyebrows, checking your skin surface and painting lips, but never for a full face make-up.

The light you work in is crucial. The rule is to apply make-up in the light it is intended for. Natural daylight is the easiest to work in, but you may need to make compensations for different environments. Artificial, fluorescent lighting drains colour from the face, so needs balancing with warm tones – shades in the brick, coral, amber, peach family – using stronger colour, but not heavier make-up, to counteract the lighting. Make-up applied in dim lighting can look too hard and bright in daylight, but at night when the light is softer, a stronger make-up does not look exaggerated. A simple test of your technique is to study a photograph of yourself. It shows you, more reliably than a mirror, what your make-up does for you, or what it doesn't do for you. So take action.

MAKE-UP GUIDELINES

Each product you use must be the right one for you. The choice is so large, there is no chance of not being able to find something suitable. Most complexions, except for perfect, flawless skin, are improved with some sort of foundation. The point of a foundation is to even out the skin tone, concealing any blemishes and dark shadows while still looking natural. Panstick days are over, foundation should be undetectable and an exact colour match. The skin on your wrist or back of the hand is not an accurate enough match to the face, so always test the foundation on your face, over clean, unmade-up skin. If you cannot find the exact shade, you can mix your own with the two nearest colours, blending them in the palm of your hand with a touch of moisturizer. It is not extravagant to have different shades of foundation as skin does not stay the same colour all year round. For an especially sheer look, blend liquid foundation (which is less covering than a cream) or fine translucent powder with an equal quantity of moisturizer. For long-lasting coverage, the application is important. Skin must be in the right condition, freshly cleansed, toned and moisturized. When all trace of moisturizer disappears, the most effective method is to use a slightly moist cosmetic sponge and dab dots of foundation across the forehead, eyelids, nose,

Lip focus: whether you wear bright colours or natural gloss, lips need to be expertly defined with a fine brush or pencil.
Matching up your lips and nails is not essential, but it is wiser to keep within the same colour range

cheeks, chin and lips, and smooth it in quickly in that order. Always be careful to blend in the direction that facial hair grows, and to avoid any tidemarks under the chin. Dark shadows under the eyes can be lightened with a paler foundation, applied before the main colour. For a tanned look, a darker foundation is a bad idea, as your white hands and neck are instant giveaways. Instead, try a sheer tan gel smoothed over foundation, and add a subtle glow to the face by putting warm blusher where the sun catches – on temples, across the forehead and a touch on the chin.

Powder still has a rather old-fashioned image, a leftover from the days when girls used to rush off and 'powder their noses'. The product has changed since then into a virtually colourless, mostly translucent protective cover that sets foundation, mops up shine, tones down high colour and provides a base for powder blusher. The best way to apply it is with a brush or cotton wool. Pat a very fine layer softly all over the face, then dust off every excess grain with the brush or clean cotton wool.

Blusher is the make-up stage that too many people miss out, mostly due to an uncertainty of where and how to put it on. Even rosy-cheeked faces need blusher. It does more than add colour, blusher can add shape and contour to a face. It can fine down a round face, soften a long, thin face and emphasize a good bone structure. Blusher comes in powder, cream, pencil or gel form. Powder is the easiest to apply, as it goes on with a brush over translucent powder, and mistakes can be toned down more easily than the other textures. Blusher goes along the cheek bone, brushed in a downward sweep from the top of the cheeks at the hairline to the centre of the cheeks. As a guide, put the index and middle finger vertically against the nose, the edge of the outer finger marks where the blusher should stop. To look completely natural, blusher has to be blended perfectly, with a brush for powder, or a dry sponge for cream, gel or crayons. The colour will be too strong and harder to blend if you put it directly on your face, so use the back of your hand as a palette to measure the colour. When you choose a blusher, pick a shade that works naturally with your complexion. An obvious contrast to your foundation looks more like make-up than a healthy glow.

Eyes are the easiest feature to enhance, but the danger is to overdo it and kill natural expression. The make-up hits you before the eyes do and their impact is lost. Best eye make-up isn't obviously make-up, but simply makes your eyes look beautiful. Avoid hard lines. Every shadow or pencil must be smudged and blended to look a natural part of the eye, and colours should be soft and neutral. The rules of matching your eye shadow to your clothes is a myth, so is the notion that pale blue shadow is the easy answer to eye make-up. Think of subtle muted colours; a palette of greys, browns, smoky blues, khaki, dusty pinks, rusts,

Before any make-up goes on, skin must be freshly cleansed, toned and moisturized

Top models prove how cosmetic skill and expertise make all the difference to the final face

burgundy tones. Don't be confined to matching your shadow to your eyes, a different shade can play up your natural colour more effectively. With green eyes, try sand, grey, smoky blue or brown. Blue eyes need stronger colours to enhance them; try shades of rust, charcoal grey, and a smudge of violet under the eye to add brightness. Most colours work with brown eyes, but experiment with muted pinks, apricots, plum, sludgy greens or different shades of brown. What counts more than the size of eyes is their intensity – bright eyes can be more beautiful than large eyes. A quick trick is to line the inner rim of the lower lid with dark kohl pencil which makes the eyes darker and the whites brighter.

Eyes need shaping. Define the hollow of the socket with a neutral pencil, the darker the pencil, the deeper set the eye becomes. Soften any pencil lines with a matching shadow, brushing under the eye as well, to accentuate the natural shape. Eye make-up is less confusing if you understand how colour behaves. Pale, shiny or frosted shades are colours that come forward, to use where you want emphasis. Darker, matt shadows retreat and create an illusion of depth or a hollow.

Eye make-up is incomplete without mascara – some days mascara alone is enough emphasis, but eye shadow without it looks incomplete. If you hate mascara, and it does take time to apply properly, try having your eyelashes dyed in a beauty salon. (Ask for blue/black, a colour mix to brighten the whites.) Otherwise find an efficient mascara, one product where it can be worth spending a little extra. The aim is to darken, not clog up each lash, so avoid brands that promise to thicken lashes, as they contain tiny filaments that stick to the ends for a while then fall off and smudge. Resign yourself to the length and texture of your lashes – it is colour that makes the difference. Apply mascara in three very thin coats, wiping the wand with a tissue between each layer. Brush top lashes from above and below, and lower lashes from above, looking straight ahead. For a wide-eyed look, separate lashes with a dry mascara wand or small toothbrush, or if they are straight, curl them with an eyelash curler.

Lipstick is a very personal cosmetic. Some people use a special lipstick colour as a personal hallmark, and are never to be seen without their shocking pink or pillar-box red mouth. Too many people underestimate what a focus lips can be. However subtle or minimal the colour, the whole face will come alive if lips are defined. It is important to create a balance between lips and eyes; they should complement each other. If you put strong eye make-up and lipstick together, one detracts from the other. It is more effective to play up one area at a time. If you draw attention to your mouth it must be in great condition; rough, chapped lips, dark hairs on the upper lip, neglected or stained teeth are all accentuated by lipstick. Out-of-condition lips are best kept natural, just outlined with soft brown pencil and brushed with clear gloss.

Many people abandon the idea of lipstick because they eat it off so quickly, or leave it smeared across a glass. The secret of long-lasting, non-smudge lipstick is in the application. The best base is foundation lightly dusted with powder, then outline the lips with a lipbrush or soft pencil, fill in with a matching lipstick or the same pencil, blot firmly with a tissue to set the colour and repeat the fill-in stage. To add shine, brush a stroke of clear gloss in the middle of the lower lip. The brighter the colour, the more striking the lips become. Pale, frosted colours make thin lips look fuller, and dark, matt colours, especially plum and dark red shades, make full lips look thinner. The various ways of altering the natural line of the mouth do need to be expertly practised, and any changes must be fractional. For seductive, pouting lips add a touch of dark brown pencil just under the centre of the lower lip. For smiling lips, erase the corners of the mouth with foundation or a skin tone concealer stick. To counteract a square face, treat lips as a triangle, and to widen a long face, extend the natural line of the lips with a fine brush or pencil stroke.

FROM DAY TO NIGHT

However carefully you make up your face in the morning, it will require some fixing by lunchtime. You need a portable prop kit to deal with minor repairs, which should include a concealer stick for unexpected blemishes, a compact of compressed translucent powder to check shiny patches, cotton buds to remove specks of eye make-up, foundation to cover the smudges, a colour pencil to brighten under the eye, and lip equipment to repair your mouth.

At night faces can take more colour. Brighter, stronger make-up becomes a vital part of an evening look – an accessory that creates a definite sense of dressing up. A night make-up accentuates the glamour of party clothes, but changing the face is also a way of moving from day to night without changing your clothes. Stronger make-up means more intensity; deeper, brighter colours, some shine, gleam and sparkle. You decide how far to take it, but the application must be perfect, with every colour blended smoothly, and no hard lines anywhere. Eyes can be dramatized with bright flashes of colour. Try drawing violet or cobalt-blue pencil along the inner rim of the eye. (Warming the pencil tip near a flame softens the point and produces a deeper, more permanent colour.)

For party eyes, brush neutral shadow across the lids, winging softly out to the temples and under the eye, then add a touch of frosted, highlight shadow (gold, pale pink, or pearl) in the centre of the top lids. Use a subtle slick of golden highlighter on the brow bone, never stark white which is too obvious and changes your natural expression. Use the same shadow to highlight shoulders, cleavage and collarbone, brushing it where the light catches. Stroke frosted blusher on cheeks and on temples, try a touch down the middle of the nose and chin, but always blend well. Set the shine with a light dusting of glimmer (or nonglimmer) translucent powder. Be daring with lip colours and experiment with bolder shades, especially if you wear natural lips during the day. But beware of overplaying the dazzle. There must be a balance between eyes, lips, cheeks and nails. Alternate the area you focus on: with iridescent lips, tone down your eye make-up and leave off the sparkle; with brilliant eyes, keep your mouth and cheeks in a soft matt colour. To add instant sparkle to everyday products, buy a pot of gold or silver glitter. Dip a glossed lipbrush into the glitter, or drop a tiny amount over your lashes as the mascara is drying, or stroke a few specks over eyelids, cheeks or freshly painted nails. An alternative for night nails is to paint a thin coat of frosted polish over your day colour.

HANDS AND FEET

Beautiful **hands and nails** are other details that count as much as the rest of your appearance. To look good they need to be healthy, which means regular pampering. Constant care is more beneficial than an occasional manicure, however thorough. But if nails are in bad shape, a beauty salon manicure can restore them to a passable condition. It is pointless to let nails grow too long; besides looking ugly, they are more likely to split and are difficult to keep in a natural oval shape. Imperfect nails can be concealed with coloured polish which, if used with a base coat, is not harmful and can strengthen and protect the nails. If you wear polish, every nail must be immaculate, there are few things more ugly than chipped fingernails. For a professional finish, apply the polish in three thin coats, letting each one dry completely. Paint each nail with three vertical strokes – one down the middle, then one either side. If you prefer natural nails, use a clear polish, or pale shell pink, or forget about colour and shine your nails with a chamois buffer and line the tips with a white nail pencil.

The rule of matching lip and nail colour is not rigid, but it is a good idea to keep the two colours in the same range. As hands are nearer the body than the face, the nail colour needs to work with your clothes. The most versatile shades are a dusty coral pink, a pale nail pink, or the classic pillar-box red. If you have brown hands, nails look prettiest painted a frosted pale colour, which also helps to enhance brown skin. Black clothes, especially in the evening, look more striking with strong red or crimson-coloured nails.

To look their best, hands and feet need to be pampered all through the year

When they are visible, toenails need the same care and attention. If feet emerge from winter hibernation in a shameful condition it is worthwhile investing in a professional pedicure and/or a chiropody treatment. Bright red toenails look good with most open sandals or peep toes, unless you can find an exact pink, purple or red colour to match your shoes.

ECONOMIZE WITH DOUBLE-DUTY PRODUCTS

The trouble with tips about make-up is the list of products essential to achieve the look. Obviously it is in the cosmetic manufacturer's interest to sell you a separate product for every make-up stage, but it makes economic sense to use cosmetics with a double or treble life. One soft brown pencil is a great basic for outlining lips, defining brows and shaping around the eye socket. A neutral tawny, peach or rose powder blusher doubles as eye shadow (but check for sensitivity), and a soft pencil blusher can colour eyes, cheeks and lips. The other option is to buy from noncosmetic counters. Baby powder costs far less than translucent powder and, if you apply it finely, does the same job. In emergencies it is a useful dry shampoo as well. Vaseline jelly is also multipurpose; it shines and conditions lips, adds a slick of gloss to straggly eyebrows, a subtle gleam to cheekbones, and some say it encourages eyelashes to grow.

Getting the maximum from cosmetics means using every ounce of each product. When a lipstick breaks in half, you can salvage it by softening the ends over a flame, joining them together and then leaving them in the fridge to set. A lipbrush is invaluable for rescuing the last of a lipstick. Dried up eye and lip pencils can be softened overnight by putting them point down in a jar containing an inch of baby oil. Mascara is past its best after six months, but can be improved by dipping the wand end of the case into very hot water for five minutes. Old nail varnish can be unclogged temporarily with the same hot-water treatment. Cakes of powder blusher or eye shadow that start to crumble can be ground into loose powder and decanted into small jars or glass salt shakers – a good way to create original colours.

The last word is for **scent** – a necessary luxury that makes you feel special. Discreet wafts of quality scent create an aura that is an elusive blend of glamour, femininity and style. Let it be a daily treat, not something to hoard for red-letter days. Buying scent is an extravagant luxury, so persuade other people to give you the one you love. Alternatively remember that Madame Chanel insisted, 'luxury is a necessity which starts where necessity ends'.

Indulge in your favourite scent – a necessary luxury

CHARACTERS IN FASHION

W hen it comes to individual style, it is easy enough to put other people into neat categories, but where do you fit in? Do you identify with any of these twelve fashion characters, or recognize your fashion traits overlapping into several of them? It is not a hard and fast list of permanent looks, more of a lighthearted rundown of independent styles that live through the volatile flights of fashion. Most of these characters seem to own an indigestibly extensive wardrobe because they represent the archetype of a style. For real-life dressing each one definitely requires a certain amount of watering down with some unpredictable individuality, otherwise the final impression will be overpoweringly fashion conscious.

THE CLASSIC COLLECTOR

She is a sensible, calculating dresser. She knows her style instinctively and stays with it. Her priorities are quality, classic clothes that never date. She prefers to wait until sale time to scoop up top-quality bargains. Her wardrobe consists mostly of separates which work together to create maximum fashion mileage; such as classic silk and cotton shirts (some are five years old, but still look right), in plain colours, stripes, small checks and polka dots. Knitwear is purely classic: V-necks, crew necks, cardigans in Shetland, lambswool and sale-bargain cashmere, which work beautifully with grey flannel and corduroy trousers, traditional kilt and an invaluable navy wool gaberdine jacket and skirt – bought as a suit but interchangeable with other separates. (The jacket works at night with silk or velvet trousers and a satin tie-neck blouse.) Her coats are everlasting: a navy wool, double-breasted classic and a buff cotton Burberry trench for the rain. Predominant colours are navy, camel, burgundy, cream, grey and white – a variety of colour and print in the

The Classic Collector: fashion mileage with her timeless coat, kilt and knits

shirts and knitwear add extra spark. Her favourite accessories: narrow leather belts, cashmere scarfs, silk squares, soft kid gloves. Her shoes: leather courts in black, navy, chocolate brown and bronze, red leather summer mules, navy and white loafers, gold strappy sandals and flat, tan leather pumps. In summer she wears bare legs and in winter neutral or black sheer tights. She carries one medium-sized navy leather bag in winter and a beige canvas and leather holdall in summer. When dressing up she changes to a small black satin evening purse. (For extra special occasions she *does* own a little black dress.) Favourite and permanent jewellery is a string of pearls, a gold chain bracelet and gold stud earrings – all given to her rather than bought.

Like her clothes, she has got her make-up down to a fine art. She uses efficient, multipurpose products, carried around with her for discreet repairs and rapid evening transformations. Her scents are Chanel No. 5 by day, Arpège by night. Her hair is well cut every six weeks (she has a standing appointment at the hairdresser's) into a minimum-fuss shape – not surprisingly groomed and versatile, like her approach to fashion.

THE EXECUTIVE DRESSER

She is related to the Classic Dresser, but the key difference is an impulsive extravagance. Her resolutions at budgeting fail, so she tends to abandon good intentions and live dangerously. The style revolves round her job. She is a career girl in a man's world and dresses in a discreetly glamorous style. (Her screen heroines are Faye Dunaway in *Network* and Jane Fonda in *The China Syndrome*.) Her clothes wrap and tuck rather than zip and button, with an enviable ease. Her look is calculatedly understated but alluring. She spends her budget on appearance, top to toe: on skin-care products, at the hairdresser's, in the beauty salon on facials, manicures, pedicures, leg waxes, suntans – her idea of bliss is a week away from the telephone in a health farm.

Her favourite clothes happen to be the sort that demand dry-cleaning. They are soft-shaped, informal classics in sophisticated fabrics: loose, unstructured silk, linen, fine wool and suede cardigan jackets and double-breasted shirts that fall open to give disingenuously intentional décolletages; dressing-gown dresses and wrap skirts that show the desired expanse of leg more unobtrusively than an overt slit. Favourite colours are impractical cream, white, beige, pale peach and camel. She too collects V-neck cashmere sweaters, and white tee shirts which are discarded the minute they lose their newness. Her only coat is a well-worn cotton trench, and while it is at the cleaners she takes taxis to stay warm and dry.

The Executive Dresser: an impulsive extravagance that favours a Calvin Klein wardrobe

Footwear is hopelessly impractical. Regardless of the weather she wears open suede sandals or peep-toe shoes, with sheer ten-denier stockings in winter and bare brown legs in summer. She is addicted to accessories, collecting quantities of expensive belts, bags, shoes, leather luggage and plain silk squares, but only wearing a few at a time. Her jewellery is minimal, just one gold high-tech watch (preferably a Rolex), and perhaps two wooden bangles or copper earrings. She is an expert make-up artist, and never looks obviously made-up, just polished. Her nails are painted a pale shell pink or buffed to a natural shine. Her attitude is flexible: some days she leaves off make-up altogether, but never goes without her spray of Private Collection scent – duty free when possible. She is incapable of travelling, which she does frequently, without a large amount of personal gadgetry. Her essentials are a travel iron, hairdryer, alarm clock, face packs, mineral water, fresh fruit and credit cards.

THE VAMP

There is nothing discreet or casual about the vamp approach; quite the opposite. She dresses to attract attention in the most deliberately dramatic and sexy manner possible. Even the postman cannot be met without an outside face – the gloss she paints on for the world to see. She is either dressed up ready for an audience, or firmly having a night in, with Bryan Ferry on the stereo or *Cabaret* on the video, probably in her satin dressing gown and a safe amount of make-up in case she is forced to answer the door bell. She would never risk being caught with a face pack on. Make-up is her seduction, without it she feels naked.

The vamp comes to life around midday, stimulated by several cups of strong black coffee – she is definitely a night person. Her characteristic smouldering eye make-up, dark glossy lips, long red nails, shining mane of hair and precariously high heels are the life and soul of every party. (She turns other girls into wallflowers and men into jelly.) She has the nerve to take her clothes one step further than anyone else dares to go. The slit in her skirt is that much higher, the skirt itself is that much shorter, her cleavage is more blatantly exposed and her jeans tighter than any one else's. She is constantly aware of her figure and on a permanent, curve-conscious diet – but one that allows cocktails.

Her favourite shapes are fitted, forties-style suits that accentuate her trim waist and curvy hips, boned, bustier tops, and anything strapless. She dresses in sensuous materials; soft, but invariably imitation, satins, chamois, crepe de Chine, velvet, and she pounces on anything sequinned or fringed. Favourite colours are black, white, bright purple, shocking

The Vamp: dressed up to kill at all times

pink and gold. Her essential accessories are outrageously tarty shoes, exotic lacy underwear (preferably black), fishnet and sheer black seamed stockings, fresh flowers, pillbox hats with veils, diamanté jewellery, ostentatious rings, feather boas and an unmistakable spicy scent, Opium or Cinnabar. She hates coats because they obstruct her appearance, although she would tolerate a silver fox fur from an admirer. Whatever the weather she wears dark glasses by day, for effect and to soothe a hangover. But she would never dream of soothing her feet with flat shoes.

THE COLLEGE GIRL

She wears young, classic clothes with a clean-cut, campus style. The basics are simple chain and sport-store separates, everything in fresh, pure colours and natural fibres to suit an active outdoor life. She feels uncomfortable in dressed-up clothes and prefers casual things. But she is always immaculately turned out with all her clothes ironed and starched before they go on. Her staple wardrobe is crew-neck Shetlands and golfer cardigans (basic colours: yellow, red, pink, navy, white), sleeveless lambswool pullovers, sweatshirts, round-neck tee shirts (several sporting Snoopy or Charlie Brown), short-sleeve polo shirts with little fine-knit collars, plain and striped Oxford cotton 'Ivy League' shirts with button-down collars (favourite colours: blue, white, pale pink and primrose). The shirt collar is *always* tucked into the sweater. Her skirts and trousers are well cut and last like good friends, improving once worn in. She chooses corduroy jeans, bleached, pastel cotton dungarees to wear with a narrow belt (she has a special white pair for evening), painter's jeans, Bermuda shorts, tracksuits, a knee-length cotton drill skirt for summer, a warm kilted skirt with woolly tights for winter. Her jacket is a school-style blazer in traditional tweed, grey flannel, candy-striped seersucker or faded, madras-plaid cotton. On cold days it's a navy duffel with a tartan lining or a traditional green loden coat, ribbed wool hat, muffler and bright Shetland gloves.

Shoes are flat penny loafers, tasselled moccasins, tennis shoes or coloured running shoes. She hates high heels and wears white or pink moccasins at night for parties, although she'd prefer to go to a *James Bond/Superman/Flash Gordon* film followed by a late night cheeseburger and milkshake.

Her favourite accessories are white and pastel coloured socks, bright leather and stretch snake belts, capacious canvas tote bags, a black diver's watch, tartan hair ribbons and a plain gold chain that she never takes off. Her beauty routine is kept simple, and to a small budget: conscientious skin care, night and morning, and minimum make-up

The College Girl: in country, campus style

Cowgirl Country: out on the range in full Western kit – sheepskin, leather jeans, moccasins, bootlace necktie, Arizona stetson

(just blusher, lip gloss, a splash of Charlie scent with a summer suntan from outdoor sports). Her hair is a straight, shoulder-length bob tied with one of her ribbons.

THE COWGIRL

A female answer to cowboy style. The look is derived from the Wild West and translated into an everyday interpretation of tough, cowboy clothes, put together to match her lifestyle. It's a look that adapts itself to smart, city life as well as home on the range. She can take the style as far as she likes; an authentic cowgirl from head to boot, or just a hint of the West.

This particular cowgirl is fairly far gone. Her style revolves mainly around denim. She owns several pairs of straight and tapered classic Western jeans, each pair lovingly faded to different shades of denim blue. She hunts for one brand name that suits her, and stays with it. She likes jeans to be comfortable, to fit without restricting. She only buys them if they are the right length, as a hem spoils the shape. On top she wears a mansize jeans jacket with the collar turned up and the sleeves rolled back. (When they wear out she chops the sleeves off to make an alternative summer waistcoat.) As a change from jeans she has a denim skirt that has to spend some time in the washing machine being softened and aged before she wears it.

Her shirts are traditional blanket check and tartan-wool, lumberjack style with neat, pointed collars, back yokes, press studs or mother-of-pearl buttons. She really prefers shirts to sweaters but keeps a few earthy coloured Shetlands.

Major investments are a three-quarter sheepskin coat, a fringed suede or leather jacket, leather jeans, and as many cowboy boots as she can afford. Favourite colours are sandy desert tones of brown, brick, olive, ginger, ochre and black.

She does have some surprisingly feminine moments in tiered, check cotton skirts in summer, and full suede skirts with jean detail stitching in winter. She wears her day style at night, substituting for a check shirt a white silk or cotton shirt with a touch of lace or embroidery. Accessories are vital to the look. She chooses bright colours and flashes of silver to lift the neutrals. Her cowboy boots come in sand, white, red, pale blue, black, some plain and workmanlike, others with extravagant stitching and appliqué. When it is too hot for boots, she changes to soft, beaded, white Indian moccasins and bare legs. Her cowboy belts are silver tipped and buckled in every collectable colour.

She loves silver and turquoise antique jewellery, tiny drop earrings, heavy bangles and genuine silver corners for shirt collars. She carries a fringed, tan suede bag, large enough to hold a change of accessories when she goes straight out from work in the evening.

She is a cinema addict, devoted to all Westerns for their escapist value and for their source of fashion inspiration. Her musical tastes are predictably in line with her Western style: Bob Dylan, Bruce Springsteen, Emmy Lou Harris and Linda Ronstadt. The switch from a day to night look is subtle. She softens the image with her invaluable accessory – make-up – transforming her fresh, scrubbed face into a delicate, English-rose complexion, and piling her long, tousled hair into a soft knot on top.

THE LAND GIRL

She buys as much as possible from government surplus stores and mixes bargain finds with inexpensive bits and pieces picked up in men's departments, jumble sales and an occasional pukka fashion shop. Although she cannot exactly wear the clothes for the purpose for which they were intended, her look bears an essentially workmanlike style. Day or night, they are not the kind of clothes for lounging about in. They spell action. The Land Girl is always on the move, tearing about on a motorbike or striding out with her cassette pack and headphones tuned in to Blondie or early Rolling Stones.

The rewarding side of Land Girl dressing is the untapped potential. You cannot categorize the look because each time she forages through a surplus store she may unearth a brand-new batch of unworn naval, army, airforce, cavalry or caterers' uniforms. The best finds are one-offs, things in limited quantities, or old stock, as they guarantee an originality. To avoid the passé surplus look, the Land Girl has to know how much surplus is too much, and where to stop. The essential ingredient to her look is large doses of wit and the unexpected. Neutral, camouflage colours look dead without an interruption of pure white and delicate pastels, which become the vital back-up to the style.

Allowing for inevitable variations, the basic Land Girl wardrobe goes something like this: khaki cotton fatigue trousers and knee-length shorts, corduroy or canvas jodhpurs with lace-up cuffs, straight baggy button-fly cord trousers. Summer staples include white cotton drill fatigues and shorts to wear with starched cotton or aertex blouses. Her coat is a sandy beige padded combat jacket – warm and waterproof. She buys woolly socks, thick leather belts, dishcloth scarves, sturdy hiking boots, canvas rucksacks, khaki tee shirts, white singlets and string vests from surplus stores, but discards anything too stamped with the uniform look – like camouflage-printed, braided and medallioned jackets, military-issue sweaters and army greatcoats. She is permanently on the

The Land Girl: down-to-earth style in surplus trousers, sturdy boots, crisp cotton blouse and a surprise suede sash

look out for a flying suit in mint condition, and Girl Guide or Boy Scout uniforms that fit. Her system is to leave the surplus clothes as she finds them – apart from laundering and starching – and add unrelated clothes to dilute the uniform style. With the khaki fatigues or jodhpurs she wears a frilly shirt or pale, cable-knit Shetland. (When the trousers are voluminous she keeps her top half neat and tucked in at the waist.) She loves pastel handknits in wool or cotton to go with thick, cord trousers and a surprise belt. She always defines her waist with something unpredictable – like a scarlet cowgirl belt, a narrow gold rouleau, a leopard-spotted suede or bronzed leather sash, a striped canvas tie or assorted scarves.

Footwear is flat but never clumpy. She likes leather or canvas lace-ups with thick socks, white ballet shoes with bare legs, or tan leather open sandals with natural toenails. A nurse's watch threaded on ribbon as a necklace is her only jewellery.

At night she changes into her smartest, most special finds. Perhaps her cream buckskin breeches and ruffled silk blouse, or if she is lucky, a white flying suit tied with a bronze belt. Make-up helps her to feel dressed up, but she always keeps it low-key with soft eye colours, brown mascara, a slick of lip gloss and a waft of Eau Sauvage.

THE COUNTRY GIRL

Her wardrobe is dictated by the environment. She needs practical clothes that keep out the cold, wind and rain; clothes that can stand up to country life, in easy-upkeep, natural fibres. By necessity it is a trouser and gumboot life a lot of the time. Her wintery clothes lean towards earthy browns and greens in traditionally British materials – tweed, corduroy, a touch of moleskin, and every kind of knitting.

Starting with the first layers, most Country Girls have a supply of white thermal underwear (in summer the vests double as tee shirts), then a selection of warm Viyella or thick cotton shirts in classic checks, plaids and pyjama stripes. The sweater drawers are crucial; country knits need to come in different sizes so one can be layered on top of the other and peeled on and off depending on the weather. She has polo necks, cardigans, V-necks, crew-necks and enormous thick arans, tweedy wool, oiled sailing or skiing jerseys as warm, top layers. This Country Girl spends the long winter evenings spinning local fleeces into yarn, to knit into huge woolly sweaters, mittens and everlasting mufflers.

Trousers are denim jeans, corduroys, tweeds or moleskins (from the local farm supply stores). When she wears a skirt it is a tweed or corduroy dirndl, full enough to climb stiles and fences, or more practical still,

The Country Girl: close to nature dressing in warm knitted layers

woollen culottes. Her coats: a tweed classic with no trace of fashion detail, a thornproof, Barbour jacket, a proper riding mac, and, beside the sea, an oilskin and yellow sou'wester. When not in her green gumboots, she wears flat, slip-on loafers, punched leather walking shoes or riding boots.

Other essentials are thick, woolly tights in bright and subdued colours, argyll, tartan and plain ribbed socks, tweed caps, trilbies, mohair scarfs, blanket shawls (otherwise used as the car rug), and gloves of every description. Her large canvas fishing bag contains lifesaving moisturizer, handcream, lipsalve, hairbrush and spray of L'Air du Temps.

For smarter, wintery days and informal evenings she chooses pretty knitwear – an angora cardigan with crystal buttons, or a pastel sweater with a bow to tie at the neck. In summer she swops warm, practical clothes for a more pastoral Kate Greenaway look. She loves fresh, sprigged cottons in bright and faded Liberty-style prints: tiered skirts edged with pintucks or broderie anglaise, flower-printed shirts with peter-pan collars, puff sleeves and narrow cuffs, drawstring smocks that hang over thin, cotton trousers. She protects her favourite clothes with a long, flowery apron – essential for gardening, picking fruit, making jam and baking bread. When it rains she changes from espadrilles into gumboots, throws on the nearest raincoat and cotton headsquare, and lets the rain fall on her face.

THE PEASANT GIRL

She shops exclusively in genuine ethnic sources, mixing the prettiest, most colourful separates into her own national costumes. She delights in jumbling the countries together, putting an Indian skirt with a Peruvian sweater, under a Russian shawl. She combines unexpected patterns and textures, basing her look around the brightest colours and richest embroidery and appliqués. Whenever she goes abroad to a good hunting ground, she takes an extra, empty suitcase for her finds. She avoids tourist souvenir shops and scours the backstreets for authentic local supplies. The Peasant Girl is something of an all-round crank, treating her food, fashion and health with a single-minded reverence. She is a vegetarian gourmet, ready to spend hours concocting exotic, whole-food banquets, medicinal herb teas or natural-recipe skin-care products. Her greatest joy is finding a source of antique, ethnic treasures: a grandmother's trunk of frail, exotic, embroidered blouses, a sumptuous Chinese dressing gown, even pieces of foreign cloth that can be adapted into a belt, a scarf, or incorporated into another garment. Fortunately the Peasant Girl can sew reasonably well. She tends to dress in layers,

The Peasant Girl: scouting the ethnic trail

partly because most of her clothes are thin cotton, worn velvet or silk and she doesn't own a practical coat, and partly because it is the best system for showing off the bright mix of colours and patterns.

Her wardrobe consists of embroidered cotton and silk blouses, smocks, boleros, appliquéd felt jackets which stop high above the shirts, skirts of every description and colour, gathered to below the knee; saris, sarongs, shawls, huge scarves which double as dresses, skirts and turbans; harem pants, muslin and calico drawstring bloomers, bright, woven rugs and shawls which alternate between wall hangings and cloaks. Her footwear: soft leather, cuffed boots on flat soles; velvet embroidered slippers; Chinese satin bar shoes; espadrilles with ribbon laces; leather flip flops and thonged gladiator sandals. Her vital accessories: assorted belts in fringed, beaded and appliquéd leather; lengths of batik tied around the waist, hips and head; silken cords with tassels; ropes of woven raffia.

Her jewellery – rings, brooches, earrings, beads, bangles – comes in homespun and natural materials like wood, leather, coins, pottery, feathers and silks.

When dressing up (hopefully for a fancy dress party or a trip to an ethnic restaurant), she wears her most exotic, brightest clothes, releases her preplaited (vegetable-dyed) hair into a crinkly, voluminous halo, accentuates her eyes with black and green kohl pencils, and splashes on her special-occasion patchouli oil.

THE JUMBLE GIRL

Her Granny style springs from a tiny budget and a feeling for nostalgia. Everything, except her underwear, is second-hand. Some things qualify as antiques, others are recent cast-offs, picked up for a few pence in a jumble sale. This astute waif haunts every kind of old clothes source: charity shops, market stalls, auctions and bazaars. But she is one of the most imaginative and discerning shoppers, with a well-trained eye to see the potential in things that others discard as old rags. She saves part of her small budget for professional repairs and dry-cleaning.

Her favourite finds are the second-hand classics: slender tea dresses in printed rayon crepe, artificial silk or faded cotton, trimmed with a narrow lace collar and delicate buttons; well-kept, pale wool beaded cardigans, to wear over the dresses or alone as an evening top; tweeds softened with wear, particularly neat, fitted jackets with velvet lapels, loose tent coats which she improves and updates by changing the usual garish buttons; or ruched cotton fifties bathing dresses. Her dream is to find a genuine thirties evening dress in crepe de Chine, panne velvet or

Jumble Girl treasure: an antique lace petticoat

beaded silk chiffon – ideas inspired by a passion for old films, particularly slushy Hollywood musicals and romantic weepies starring Joan Crawford, Greta Garbo or Bette Davis. Until then she compromises with a glamorous satin and lace petticoat, dressed up with an old fur stole. She loves fine lace and buys separate antique lace collars and cuffs to liven up the basic jumble. She wears a faded patchwork skirt – once a bedspread – with a favourite sweater or a lacy wool cardigan with tiny pearl buttons.

In second-hand sources she hunts for low-heeled Granny shoes with a button bar, classic sixties pumps and old-fashioned tap shoes. Or she buys low satin court shoes from bridal departments and dyes them different colours. She wears opaque, sixty-denier nylon, wool, lisle or cotton stockings – bought mostly from small-town haberdashers. If she cannot find the right colour to match her clothes, she dyes white tights instead.

She always wears an assortment of junk and semiprecious jewellery: dangly earrings, strings of beads, bracelets and brooches. She loves Victorian and Art Deco styles, and anything in moonstone, crystal, opal, garnet or pearl, cameo brooches, and hat pins to use like stick pins in the lapels of a jacket. She collects lace shawls and long silk scarves to knot at the waist or loop around her neck like Isadora Duncan.

Luggage consists of an old Gladstone bag and several original fifties and sixties stamped leather and patent handbags with short, curved handles. At night she carries a beaded, satin purse on a long gilt chain containing a compact, a twenties cigarette holder and lace handkerchief. Like the clothes, her make-up is old-fashioned. She is a lipstick and powder girl and her scent is rosewater or lavender essence. She keeps her soft, wavy hair freshly washed, tied like Alice with a velvet bow, or swept back with antique slides and combs.

THE ROMANTIC

The Romantic: frilled white Victoriana with tough brown leather and the essential straw panama

At first glance she could be called an eccentric, even a mess. But she has an extremely feminine style all of her own. She treats clothes in a witty, non-conformist way and puts them all together like a connoisseur, using instinct instead of convention. Her approach to fashion is an extension of her personality. Beneath the scatty, unpunctual surface she is a well-read, occasionally intimidating bluestocking with fixed opinions on politics, the law, the media, the arts. She has an élitist attitude to the cinema, criticizing anything other than an obscure foreign film, or one involving her intellectual pin-up, Woody Allen. It has to be said that *Annie Hall* was a catalyst for her individual, if slightly contrived, style.

She keeps an eye on fashion and takes the parts she likes and ignores

the rest. Her other and more important sources are antique shops selling Victorian white cotton clothes, and menswear departments. She is a romantic mixture of starched white frills and tough tweeds, using the hallmarks of male dressing – a tweed jacket, a thick, brown belt, a bow tie, stripey braces, a heavy watch – to dispel any chance of a chocolate-box image. The style is seasonless, based mainly on cotton which means more layers in winter, fewer in summer and in the evening. Her Victorian underwear – the bloomers, camisoles, lace blouses, nightshirts – are the winter underlayers; she puts a warm, man's cardigan or tweed jacket with a velvet collar over a lace camisole or frilly shirt. Over her pin-tucked petticoat or mid-calf bloomers, she wears a flower-printed, brushed cotton skirt.

Her best summer dress is a white Victorian nightshirt which becomes a blouse worn under an extra skirt in winter. She wears men's silk-backed waistcoats over her frilliest shirts, men's check shirts with her frothiest petticoats, and always a thick, brown belt with a heavy brass buckle. Her most extravagant buys are irresistible Fair Isle handknits which she wears as a change from the standard white blouses.

She completely loses her head over delicious coloured, usually wildly impractical, but beautiful shoes – which come out at night. By day she feels more at home in ballet shoes, flat pumps with bows, brown leather sandals, or gumboots. She loves patterned and textured tights and uses them as an extra warm layer under the cottons.

Accessories are an essential part of the appearance: a man's felt trilby or straw panama hat; a red spotted handkerchief for daytime, a lace-edged cotton one at night; horn-rimmed spectacles worn on a chain for safe keeping. No other jewellery except her gold grandfather watch on a well-worn, brown leather strap.

She washes her long hair constantly, leaving it to dry naturally – sometimes piling it inside a hat or tucking it behind a cotton gipsy scarf. Scent is a vital extravagance – she treats herself to Diorissimo soap, dusting powder, bath oil and perfume spray. Make-up is saved for the evenings. She spends hours perfecting her eyes, and a favourite but time-consuming trick is to thread a bright pink or scarlet ribbon through the neck of a white camisole and then paint her lips exactly the same colour.

THE GROWN-UP TOMBOY

The Grown-Up Tomboy: at home in the most conventional menswear

She prefers the comfort and quiet style of menswear. Her look is mannish, but never butch. She takes the clothes that are not exclusively masculine, the least designed, most traditional classics that convert naturally into female wear. The fabrics are typical of the most conservative menswear: pinstripe suitings, cotton shirting, linen, tweeds, flannel, gaberdine, corduroy, suede, leather, discreetly patterned knits – but whenever possible the Tomboy chooses feminine colours. She is not rigidly opposed to female clothes, but likes the cut and roominess of genuine menswear better than female clothes that imitate men's clothes.

She buys everything, except shirts, one size too large, never more because anything too outsize is unflattering. Her trousers are straight legged with pleated tops, mostly in crisp linen, needlecord and lightweight tweed. Her tops are white tee shirts, piped pyjama jackets and endless permutations of soft-collared and collarless, striped cotton shirts. Knitwear is assorted cable-knit Shetlands, lambswool V-necks and chunky cardigans in white, cream, camel, pale blue, grey, pale pink and yellow. Fair Isle waistcoats and slipovers take the place of a man's pinstripe waistcoat, which is too blatantly masculine. Coats are true men's classics: an oversized cotton trench (as worn by favourite film star Humphrey Bogart), a herringbone tweed hacking jacket and a simple, suede windcheater. When she wears a skirt it is a traditional kilt or a straightish pinstripe, which go together with flat-heeled, leather boots or ribbed tights and low, leather loafers.

Shoes are her greatest concession to femininity, mostly low heeled, but elegant and prettily coloured. She loves patent pumps, pale suede lace-ups and correspondent walking shoes. For parties she wears a black tuxedo with high-heeled, bronze sandals. (She hires a white tuxedo for very special occasions.) Her favourite accessories are large, paisley wool scarves that she ties loosely round her shoulders over a jacket. She collects narrow leather and suede belts in every colour, has drawers full of cotton and wool socks (some Argyll checked, but mostly plain colours). She tends to use her pockets in place of a handbag – most Tomboys are self-disciplined and reduce their personal clutter to a minimum. Her jewellery is a permanent fixture: classic gold rings, pearl stud earrings and one mansize, mix metal watch on a silver link strap. She treats make-up and scent (Empreinte or Calèche) as everyday essentials, and uses muted neutral colours day and night. Her hair is simple, either long and smooth or cut short, but always soft and feminine to compensate for any severe tailoring and masculine lines in her clothes.

THE POP GIRL

She is a fashion butterfly, hopping from one pop style to another, settling on the look that matches the newest musically inspired cult. She may be a discotee, a rocker, a punk, or an aggressive feminist, depending on the feeling in the air. Some pop styles are fashion innovations, others are

The Pop Girls: darting from one new wave to the next

recycled revivals from the fifties, sixties and seventies. The vibes oscillate between aggression, energy, nostalgia, escapism and excitement, and the Pop Girl moves with them. As a disco girl she wears skin-tight satin or shiny Spandex jeans with a clinging tee shirt or spangly, stretch boob tube, leotards, satin shorts, skating skirts, shiny footless tights, sequinned belts, high-heeled dancing sandals. She shines with hot, luminous colours, her face sparkles with silver disco glitter and iridescent make-up. As a fifties rockabilly, she turns to *West Side Story*, full-blown skirts, sleeveless high-school blouses with little collars, Hawaiian-printed bowling shirts, snug side-buttoning pedal pushers, white ankle socks, flat little dance pumps and ponytails.

In the wake of Suzi Quatro, Debbie Harry and Chrissie Hynde she becomes a female New Wave rocker. She wears a leather motorbike jacket, heavy with zips and studs, leather jeans or washed-out, tight denim ones, perhaps a zip-up mini with black fishnet stockings, leather boots, black lace mittens, ragged hair and black eye make-up – hidden by Easy Rider sunglasses. Occasionally she adds a strategically placed cosmetic bruise. She may stray back into punk with graffittied knotted tee shirts, vinyl trousers and jackets, heavy silver chains, safety-pin necklaces, multi-coloured spiky hair and theatrically aggressive war paint.

Or she may revamp the psychedelic sixties with a colourful jumble of flower-power Carnaby Street gear. Home-made minis from floral curtains, jumble sales or children's shops, teamed with clashing paisley and polka-dot blouses – the sort with long, pointed collars and wide, flyaway cuffs – possibly a luminous kipper tie worn as a belt. She hunts for authentic sixties sleeveless polo necks with zips at the back, printed wool and mohair sweaters, op art shifts and minis, and pearlized, patent leather pumps. Her hair is teased into a modern beehive, face paled with white foundation and baby powder, accentuated by stark black eyeliner and pale pink frosted lipstick.

Or she may escape as a 'new romantic' – the swashbuckling breed who react against everyday monotony and violence by diving into fancy dress. The heroes are pirates, highwaymen and brave Byronic sea captains, whose uniforms inspire the fantasy clothes. Everything is light-hearted, flamboyant, and anything goes: ruffles, frills, lace scattered over piratical breeches, brocade waistcoats, gold-braided Captains' jackets. All a characteristically non-conformist mix of pattern and colour.

ACKNOWLEDGEMENTS

I would like to thank everyone at Vogue who helped me with this book: especially Beatrix Miller for encouraging the idea; Alex Kroll for his enthusiasm and support; the Condé Nast book department and library for their help, research and patience. Thanks, too, to Georgina Boosey for her expert editing; Vogue Fashion Room for past and present inspiration, particularly Sheila Wetton and Anna Harvey who taught me so much about fashion, and Antonia Kirwan-Taylor for her invaluable imagination and suggestions. Finally, a special thank you to Susan Hill at Hutchinson for making this book possible.

LIST OF PHOTOGRAPHERS